SKATE MANIA

JEREMY CASE

A big thanks to Cyrus Shahrad

PUFFIN BOOKS

Published by the Penguin Group: London, New York, Australia , Canada,
India, New Zealand, South Africa

Penguin Books Ltd, Registered Offices: 80 Strand, London WC2R 0RL, England

www.penguin.com

First published 2003

1

Text copyright © Jeremy Case, 2003

Illustrations copyright © Zac Sandler, 2003

All rights reserved

The moral right of the author and illustrator has been asserted

Made and printed in England by Clays Ltd, St Ives plc

ISBN 0–141–31638–1

contents

chapter one
Just dropping in

Well done. You've got this far. Most people look at skateboarders and just see kids falling off their boards and decide it's not for them. They don't get it. But you've looked at skateboarders and instead of seeing kids falling off you've seen kids having fun. You've got the right attitude. And that's really what skateboarding is all about.

Skating is now more popular than it ever has been. It seems like the whole world wants to ride a board. Kids are skating from Russia to Brazil. (Well, not literally but there's always a first.) There are 11 million skaters in America – that's more than the population of Belgium. Well, maybe if the Belgians weren't so busy making chocolate . . . Getting into skating opens up the possibility of making new friends anywhere, in any city on the planet.

In this country, skating's everywhere too. Last year's Ozzfest in Donington Park had an extreme sports arena; there was a skate ramp at Reading Festival and attendance at the NASS extreme sports event in Bath has risen by 400 per cent in three years. In some schools, you can now skate in PE. Even Prince Charles – our future king – skated on the BBC, back in the day. But don't let that put you off. It doesn't matter who's skateboarding, or how many others are doing it. Skating is a personal challenge. It's about pushing yourself, developing your own style and conquering your fears.

This book has everything you ever need to know about skateboarding. How to do tricks, where to skate, how to take care of your board, how to build your own ramp, how to take skate photos and how to become a pro. There are chapters on fashion, videos, music and games, the shops where you can buy them, websites and a dictionary of skate terms. Plus interviews with top pros and a whole section on girl skateboarders. The only thing missing is a skateboard. You'll have to get that yourself.

But none of it will truly make sense until you get on a board and push off. Only then will you stop seeing park benches as somewhere to eat your KFC and handrails as things to help old biddies down stairs. You'll realise that the whole world's a giant, free skatepark. Suddenly the boring local high street will become the source of endless enjoyment, a challenge that needs to be tamed, an arena for the fight between man and manmade environment. That gnarly ledge might have won the battle this time, but it certainly won't win the war.

Skating's come a long way since Tony Alva first aired out of those Californian swimming pools in the '70s, but the sentiment's still the same. Now there's more prime skating territory than ever as the concrete jungle grows and grows, and more skaters to take it on. So what are you waiting for? It's time to join the urban revolution.

"I can't keep count of how many friends I've made skateboarding. Every time I go I meet someone new."
Nebil Saad, 17, South London

"You can do it just about anywhere and it's really, really fun."
Joe Ponting, 12, Wiltshire

chapter two
the history lesson

Skating's not some new-fangled craze that's going to die out by next Christmas. It's been around since way before your parents were kids. Not even eggheads know the precise date when the skateboard was invented, but they reckon it was sometime in the 1930s. American kids used to race homemade scooters, which were basically planks of wood with rollerskate wheels and a fruit crate nailed to the front for steering. This of course was in the days before PlayStation, so there was nothing better to do. One day, some forgotten hero rode right into a tree, snapped his "handlebars" off, bravely got back on his board and accidentally gave birth to skating.

Not surprisingly, riding into trees didn't catch on and it wasn't until the late '50s, when surfing began to take

California by storm, that skateboarding rode again. This time, instead of an accident, we've got the weather to thank. The surfers were bored because there was no swell, so they decided to try surfing on land. First they attached wheels to their surfboards, but being all precious and that, they were worried about breaking their sticks. So instead, they made decks out of short, four-inch-wide pieces of wood and took to the streets. And kinda liked it, man.

The craze took off and toy skateboards started to appear in shops in 1959. Problem was, you couldn't do much with them because, quite frankly, they were rubbish. The wheels were made of clay – that's, like, hard mud – the decks were heavy and there was hardly any nose or tail. Any time you hit a crack you were a goner. Give the kids credit, though – they still rode the prehistoric board like it was the latest Tony Hawk pro model. Skate company Makaha was formed and competitions were held. One of the best tricks invented at this time was the Gorilla Grip – you rode barefoot, wrapped your toes around the nose and tail and then tried to jump as high as possible. Imagine trying that the next time you go down the skatepark.

But it was all too good to be true. Despite the birth of skateboards with rubber wheels in 1965, too many kids were getting hurt trying to go far faster than their little toy skateboards would allow. Even back in those days, parents were a pain and in many US cities the "responsible adults" clubbed together and successfully banned skating. The companies that were making the boards went out of business and you couldn't buy a set-up anywhere. Skateboarding took its first big slam.

Five years on, the seaside suburbs of LA – Venice Beach, Santa Monica and Ocean Park – had become rundown and were nicknamed Dogtown. This was where a group of surfers used to hang out, daring each other to ride between the iron struts of the disused pier. They were part of the Z-Boys surf team, set up by local surfboard shop owners Jeff Ho, Skip Engblom and Craig Stecyk (no sniggering at the back, please).

As all the amusement arcades had shut down, there was nothing to do in the afternoon when the waves died down. So the juniors in the surf team – people like Stacy Peralta, Tony Alva, Jay Adams, Shogo Kubo and one girl, Peggy Oki – decided to make their own entertainment. You couldn't get skateboards down the high street any more, so they built their own using the tried and tested two rollerskate trucks and a plank of wood method.

But this time they really rode them. They took the skills they'd learnt in the sea and used them on their skateboards, carving and leaning into turns, trailing their arms and crouching down low as they sped downhill. Then they took skating back to the old school – literally. They discovered that Paul Revere Junior High had curved banks in the playground and went to skate there, weaving in and out of drinks cans. **"To a 12-year-old kid it was awesome,"** says Tony Alva. **"The banks were really smooth and pristine, just these huge, glassy waves."**

Then in 1973 someone called Frank Nasworthy did them all a massive favour by coming up with the polyurethane wheel, which is basically just a fancy name for plastic. It meant they didn't have to worry if they got their lines slightly out and ploughed into a drinks can. That slightest bump wasn't going to knock them off. Another kind and generous man called Larry Stevenson invented

the kicktail and Bennett Hijacker started making the first skateboard trucks.

Suddenly the Z-Boys could do all kinds of fast turns and swerves and developed their style even further. When they turned up at their first US skate contest in 1975, the Bahne-Cadillac National Championships, they destroyed the competition. Everyone else was doing moves from back in the '60s (imagine how your parents dance at weddings). Old skool skating was like synchronised swimming on a board – handstands, 360 spins, pirouettes and nose manuals while rolling in circles. **_It was a no-brainer._**

The following year, God decided to give skateboarding a helping push. He stopped the rains and there was a massive drought in America. Despite being really thirsty, the Z-Boys realised that the empty swimming pools in the nearby rich houses were even better than the school banks and would go and skate them when the owners were at work. It wasn't always easy to see over the millionaires' high fences, though. So one time Jay and Shogo paid for a flying lesson just so they could look for pools from the air. And you think you're keen on skating!

The vertical walls of the pools added a whole new dimension to the Z-Boys' skating and led to the world's first airs. (NB. If you ever meet anyone from San Diego, they'll claim that aerials were invented in their home town. Don't worry about it. No one really knows. Or cares.) A rich friend of the Z-Boys, Gino, was dying of cancer, and so his dad let them skate his pool to try to cheer Gino up. They called it the Dogbowl. This is where many of today's moves were born. Tony Alva pulled off the first frontside air, and lip grinds and slides were invented. Over on America's other coast, a 14-year-old kid called Alan Gelfand invented the ollie off a ramp in Florida in 1977. Rodney Mullen took it to the street, and the ollie is still the basis of all modern skate tricks.

Skating was big business and the Z-Boys went their separate ways to make their fortunes as parks were built all over America and the UK. The best thing about skateboarding was that anybody could do it. Kids of all colours, backgrounds and religions were skating together. But the good times couldn't last. In 1980, skaters stopped going to the parks. They were badly designed (ring any bells?), safety rules were too strict and they'd become too expensive and over-run with the new crazes of BMX and rollerblading. **_Skating ate dirt again._**

A hardcore of riders went back to the original streets and did their own thing for a few years. They built wooden ramps and halfpipes in back yards and car parks and moves learnt on the street were taken to vert skating. Then the first Bones Brigade video came out in 1984 and vert riding came off the ramp and into people's front rooms. A spindly kid called Tony Hawk was winning everything and Christian Hosoi, Lance Mountain, Neil Blender and Steve Caballero became household names. **_Like Fairy Liquid._**

As the '80s progressed, the return of street skating coincided with the complete abandonment of fashion sense. Mullet, anyone? Mark Gonzales and Natas Kaupas started kickflipping and ollieing so high you couldn't work out whether it wasn't really vert after all. Just to confuse us even more, girlie swot Mark Gonzales started pulling off all of his tricks "switch", so everyone had to go back to the drawing board and relearn all their moves backwards. Tech skating was born.

In the UK, the scene was finally starting to get rolling. Many concrete parks built in the '70s and early '80s

(Livingston opened in 1981) had been left abandoned as the early craze died out. But then the first dedicated skate mag, *RAD (Read and Destroy)*, was published in the mid-1980s, Slam City Skates opened in 1986 and unlikely hero Michael J Fox inspired kids the world over to skate after his sequence in *Back to the Future*. The following year, the Brit scene exploded after the huge success of demos featuring visiting US pros like Christian Hosoi and Mark Gonzales.

Then in the early '90s, kids like Jamie Thomas came out of nowhere (well, actually he came out of a 15-stair handrail) and suddenly grinds and slides came with a serious health warning. Poorly made skateboards weren't strong enough to cope with getting beaten up every day and started to break down and cry. Skating fell off the rails into intensive care in the early '90s. Kids couldn't afford to keep buying new boards and suddenly everyone was into rollerblading (will they ever learn?).

But experienced pros like Tony Hawk, Andy Macdonald and Danny Way looked after skating and showered it with a lot of love and attention. And after the Extreme Games were shown on satellite telly in 1995, skating had been nursed back to full health. In the UK *RAD* magazine morphed into *Sidewalk Surfer* (now just called *Sidewalk*) and once again Brit skaters had something they could really call their own. By the late '90s, Skate of Mind had opened its doors and *Document* magazine came out as a serious rival to *Sidewalk*.

Towards the end of the century, both types of skating made a comeback. Vert moves invented by Tony Hawk and Steve Caballero were brazenly nicked by snowboarders and no one even batted an eyelid. In the streets, Jamie Thomas and Chad Muska continued to ignore their mums' pleas and did ever larger handrails. Then one day Tony Hawk decided he'd had enough and retired, but so that no one would really miss him, he turned himself into a virtual skateboarder and launched the computer game Pro Skater. The rest, as they say, is history.

"There are no rules in skateboarding. The best and the worst can skate the same session. That doesn't happen in football. There's no winner or loser, the guy that's having the most fun is the best rider."
Tony Alva, pro skater

"It's as if when we were kids, we were infected with a virus and that virus was skateboarding. In the '70s, we went all over the world infecting kids with this virus because they were open and willing hosts."
Stacy Peralta, pro skater

"It was amazing skating the big parks in California in the early '80s. Then skateboarding was seen as a craze, like rollerblading or scooters. It lapsed for a few years and then started again. Now, finally skateboarding can look after itself. We will always be here."
Blimz, 37, Birmingham

chapter three
Buying your Board

Of course you're desperate to rush out to the skate shop. But buying a board isn't like buying a Maccy D. There are all kinds of decisions to be made and you need to make sure you're clued up before you part with your hard-swindled cash. Ask your friends about their set-ups, try them out, read magazines and ask in proper skate shops. You might find a sale or even – shock, horror – a helpful assistant. Just don't do your window shopping on a Saturday afternoon because you'll be less popular than a busted knee at the Munster World Championships. If all your friends are starting too, you might get a group discount if you all buy together. Sometimes you find cheaper gear at skate contests or get a secondhand board by checking the for-sale notices at your local skatepark. You'll need to check it's in good working order though so read the Skateboarding MOT (see page 20) before you shake on a deal with the Del Boy of the local skate community.

The first thing to decide is whether to buy a readymade board or whether to shell out a little extra and get all the parts separately. You can get really cheap boards from toy shops but they break easily and could be dangerous. Ready-assembled boards, called completes, from proper skate shops are more reliable, but it's still worth building one yourself as you'll learn how your skateboard works. That way if something goes wrong, you'll know how to fix it.

DECKS

This is what you stand on. All decks these days are made from seven sheets of Canadian maple wood glued together and pressed into a standard shape. Unlike in the animal kingdom, the nose is slightly longer than the tail – just so you don't make a fool out of yourself straightaway. It's not worth splashing out £100 on a pro deck if you're a beginner – save that for when you're training for your first contest. Established skate companies make good quality decks and UK brands are cheaper than American. So do your bit for reducing national debt and buy British – Unabomber, Blueprint, Death, Reaction, Clown, Third Foot, Panic and Icon are all homegrown. Blank decks (without graphics) are even cheaper. Customise yours with your own designs (see

Chapter 16) and be truly individual.

The most important thing is to buy a deck that's the right size for you. Lengths vary so just get one that feels right when you stand on it in the shop (if you're very young you can get a mini deck). Widths range from 7 to 8.5 inches depending on what you plan to do with your board. Narrower decks are good for tricks, whereas wider ones are more stable and better suited to vert. If it's your first deck, get something in the middle (around 7.75 inches or slightly wider) so you can ride all terrains. Finally, all decks curve down slightly in the middle (called a concave). Some people say a larger concave helps the deck grip their front foot better when they ollie, but it's all down to personal preference.

GRIPTAPE

Like sandpaper. You put it on your deck so your feet don't slip off. Unless you want them to, that is – it's not flypaper, you know. Some nice shops will give you griptape for free, especially if you're buying everything else from them. For some reason, plain griptape sticks better. Don't ask why. It's one of the mysteries of the universe.

WHEELS

Hardness and size are all important with wheels. Harder wheels are well suited for skateparks as they're faster and it's easier to ollie as you get more bounce when you push down on the board. Softer wheels mean a more comfortable ride. Smaller wheels make flip tricks easier, but larger ones allow you to go faster and over rougher ground. Wheels vary from 50 to

60mm in diameter and hardness is measured on the durometer scale. For a beginner, 55 to 58mm with a durometer of 97 would be a good starting point. Don't worry about getting brand wheels – blank ones will suit you fine.

BEARINGS

You'll need two per wheel, one inside and one out, so your wheels turn smoothly. Bearings all have ABEC ratings, but these are a bit of a red herring. Just get the cheapest ones – whoever is shelling out will thank you for it. Eight washers go between the bearings and the wheel.

TRUCKS

These are the two metal mounts for your wheels that attach to your deck and help you to carve, turn and grind. Made of cast aluminium, trucks will last longer than the rest of your set-up. Some trucks turn better and others are lighter so ask for advice in the shop. Make sure the width of your trucks is the same as the width of your deck – they should line up with the edges. In the centre of the truck, the kingpin controls the ease with which your board turns. Keep them tight and you'll be more stable, looser and you'll be able to turn faster. Your trucks take time to wear in so you'll need to adjust them as you go along. Make sure the kingpin doesn't stick out or you'll find it harder to grind.

RISERS

You mainly need risers if you've got large wheels. They are basically padding that fits between your trucks and your deck to prevent the wheels from touching the underside of your board. Risers are also shock absorbers, helping you to land tricks and keep your board from breaking, especially if you're carrying a bit of extra baggage. You have to bear in mind that they make the board heavier, so risers will slow you down.

NUTS AND BOLTS

You'll need eight of these babies. They attach your trucks to your deck. Don't screw them in too tight though, because they'll sink into the deck which will lead to cracks under the base plates. The length depends on whether you have risers. Shorty's bolts come in two different colours, so you can put the four silver ones at the front to tell the nose from the tail.

IT'S A SET-UP!
How to assemble your board

Yes, we know you're all jumped up about your new board, but don't go off bragging to your pals on your mobie until you've watched the shop assistant put everything together. Pay attention, kid! One day, you'll have to do it for yourself. But just in case you were daydreaming of your first half cab, here's the basics . . .

First, you want to stick the griptape down. Put your deck on a flat surface and peel the back layer off the griptape. Place it over the deck and lay it down smoothly, brushing out any air bubbles with a wheel. When it's all hunky-dory, you need to run a flat metal surface, like a blunt knife, around the edge of the deck, bending the griptape down as you go. You will notice a white line appears. Cut around this white line with scissors or a sharp knife – if you're a nipper, ask a parent to help. Then sand down any rough edges with a file.

Next attach the trucks one at a time. Pierce the griptape above each hole in your deck and push your four bolts through. Turn the deck over and slip the riser pad (if you have one) and then the truck over the bolts, making sure the kingpin is facing towards the centre of the deck. Tighten your nuts right up (no sniggering at the back, please) and then do the same with the other truck, again making sure the kingpin is facing towards the centre. Your trucks must be in line with each other and the deck.

Now you need to get the bearings into the wheels. Use your trucks to help you. Put one over the axle and push your wheel down on to it. Remove the wheel and check the bearing's not sticking out. Put another bearing over the axle, turn the wheel round and repeat. Then do the other three wheels. Now put a wheel on each axle and screw them in, making sure they still spin freely. When you place the board on the floor, one of the wheels might not be touching the ground. Don't lose any sleep over it. This is quite normal with new set-ups and will right itself after you've worn all the parts in.

> **"Skating's great. It's difficult landing tricks but you can improve all the time."**
> Matthew Varela, 13, Colombia

> **"I saw some friends doing it and it looked like a good way to have fun. My best trick is a kickflip."**
> Mason Collins, 14, New Zealand

FUNBOX FUNBOX FUNBOX FUNBOX
BOARDING ON THE INSANE

Over the years, skateboard companies have experimented with all kinds of weird and not so wonderful shapes and designs. Even these days, you can buy a board from Flowlab for carving down the streets like you're on a snowboard. Instead of trucks, there are seven wheels aligned in a curve at the front and back that allow you to lean through 45 degrees to really bust those turns. But that's nothing compared to the kinds of gubbins and gimmicks they've tried to foist on unsuspecting kids in the past. Decks came with scratch-off lottery card graphics, burnt-on images and velvet glued into the designs. Wheels had mini tyres or were totally round like golf balls, while others lit up when you skated. Griptape started out life as a bit of carpet stuck to the deck and spent puberty as a weird kind of glue-gravel mixture that was so sharp that kids kept cutting their hands on it. Deck shapes got particularly ridiculous in the '80s, with fishtails, foot shapes, wavy edges, crooked decks and hammerheads. And let's not forget Sky Hooks, which attached to your deck so you could slip your feet under them, or Suspenders – Velcro straps for wrapping round your shoes so you could pull off hands-free airs. If you're a cheat, that is.

www.thedeathsquad.co.uk/deathsquad/unboards.htm
More bizarre boards.

chapter four
safety

Skateboarding's dangerous. Fact. If you make it through your skating career without getting hurt at least once, you're either immortal or a liar. And the first rule, which might seem obvious but is tempting to ignore as you get better, is NOT to skate on or around busy roads where there's loads of traffic and unpredictable drivers. Secondly, warm up with some stretching exercises. This might seem a bit tedious and like you're doing an impression of your mum at yoga class, but if you don't do it, you're gonna feel it. And it'll make you a whole lot more supple to pull off those gnarly tricks. All the pros do it – honest. And finally, always wear safety gear when you're learning. Remember, if you skate safe today, you can skate again tomorrow.

Helmet Make sure it's a snug fit so it doesn't fall off. If you ever think about going on the vert ramp without a skid lid, you need your brain examining in any case.

Kneepads Should have a plastic cap for sliding so you can bail out without hurting yourself if you miss a trick (see below).

Elbow pads Chipped funnybones are a very common injury. And they ain't funny.

Wrist guards Because you always put your hands out to stop yourself when you fall. The plastic strips prevent your wrists from bending out of position even if you're double-jointed.

THE FALL GUY

FLAT

Let's face it, you're going to slam a lot when you're starting out. But if you've learnt how to fall properly, you can minimise the damage. On the flat, curl up into a ball and roll away in the direction you've come off. Keep relaxed and don't put out your hands.

RAMP

Your arms should protect your head. Try to land on your ass as it's the softest part of your body. If you're on the vert ramp, you'll need a different technique. Step off the board with your front foot, bend your knees and slide down facing forwards on your kneepads and the tops of your shoes. You should reach the bottom safe and sound. Then get straight back up there again so you don't lose your confidence.

SKATEBOARD MOT
Check your board regularly to make sure it's safe.

TRUCKS

If one truck's getting bashed more than the other, swap them over. Tighten screws and bolts once a week and the wheel nuts before each session. Pivot cups and rubber bushings are usually the first things to go. Look closely and if you see a split, get some new ones. Replace nuts and bolts that are worn out and if you see a crack in the truck itself, it's off to the skate shop immediately for you, you tearaway.

FUNBOX FUNBOX FUNBOX FUNBOX
THE ONE THAT GOT AWAY

Parents giving you grief about skating? Won't let you get a board because they think you're going to cripple yourself? Tell them that the US Consumer Products Safety Commission (1997) found that skateboarding's safer than football, golf and – get this – even fishing!

GRIPTAPE

To remove and replace old griptape, heat it up with a hairdryer to loosen the glue. Use a table knife to lever up one part so you can get a firm grip. Then put your foot on the board and pull. It should peel off in one fell swoop (unless you didn't move your foot, silly!). Keep griptape sticky by brushing it with a little water using an old toothbrush. Dry with an old rag immediately afterwards.

DECK

Sand down any rough edges or small cracks with spare griptape. Unfortunately, if a layer has started to come apart, you have to peel it off and kiss it goodbye. It's a shame as your deck won't be perfect any more, but using glue can cause new problems as it tends to expand in the wood which results in cracks. If it's happening often, consider buying a plastic tailsaver or noseguard. Pressure cracks are quite common, but ones that spread through several layers are dangerous and you should replace your deck. Don't leave a deck in a car overnight, especially in cold UK weather, as the morning dew builds up in the wood and causes the board to lose its pop. Oh, and don't ride through water. It's not a surfboard, fool!

WHEELS

If one wheel is wearing down more than the others, swap it with the one diagonally opposite. If wheels have become wobbly, tighten the nuts. Watch out for flat spots and rough edges. If there are chunks missing, empty your piggybank and get down the shop.

BEARINGS

Clean bearings every month as they get clogged up with dirt and grit. Lay some newspaper over a flat surface, take off the wheels and lever out the bearings with the truck axle. Clean them with loo roll, then lubricate both sides with oil from the

FUNBOX FUNBOX FUNBOX FUNBOX
THE RULES OF SKATING

1. Don't skate across other people's lines in skateparks.

2. Wait your turn on vert and other ramps.

3. Help younger kids if they're struggling with a trick or if they've hurt themselves.

4. Don't be rude to the public, security guards or the police or you'll ruin it for others. Be polite and reason with them. If that doesn't work, move on, tell your parents if you think they were being unfair and try again another day.

5. Skating down the high street on a Saturday afternoon is not going to make you the most popular kid on the block. So use *your* block and go back on Sunday evening when all the old fogeys are at home watching *Songs of Praise*.

6. Public buildings are tempting spots, but they're normally off-limits. So leave them alone. If you're not sure, ask some older skaters.

7. Don't trash your own spots with litter and graffiti.

8. Don't go skating at night and always skate with a group of friends. If you come across any trouble, leave it and tell your parents or the police.

9. Don't stay in one place for too long. There are always newer and better spots just waiting to be discovered.

10. Always remember that little you is representing the whole skate community. So behave all proper-like.

skate shop. Juggle the bearing round in your hand for a couple of minutes. More dirt will come out. Clean the bearing again with a fresh piece of paper. Old or worn bearings make little squeaks. If cleaning doesn't help, you need new ones.

"I've hit my elbow about eight times and it kind of starts to hurt. It doesn't put me off as you have to injure yourself to get better, you have to practise."

Charles Nicholson, 13, Balham, London

"I started skateboarding because I lived in the country and there's nothing else to do apart from climb trees. When you fall out of a tree it hurts more."

Carl Harling, 13, Vauxhall, London

chapter five
Getting Started

Who're you calling goofy?

So you've got a skateboard. The first thing to do is realise
that your life will never be the same again. Then you can
work out your stance. If you want to give your friends a
laugh, get one of them to give you a shove in the back
when you're not looking. Whichever foot you put forward
first to stop yourself falling is the one that goes at the front
of the board (if you don't know which end that is, the nose
is slightly longer than the tail). If you're on your own, put
your board on the carpet and jump on to it and see which
way is more comfortable. If it feels more natural with your
left foot forward then you're regular, if your right foot's at
the front, you're goofy. Don't worry, this doesn't mean you
need a painful trip to the dentist. Goofy is in fact perfectly

normal, like being left-footed at football. In fact, as you get better, you'll learn to do tricks in both stances anyway – this is called riding switchstance.

Next you need to get used to the feeling of being on the board. Practise on the carpet in your front room or in the back garden. That way it won't slip out from under you and the only injury you'll get is a clip round the ear when your mum discovers the grass stains on your combies. Stand on your board with your feet facing sideways. The front foot should be over the truck and at a slight angle, toes pointing forwards, and your back foot between the tail and the back truck. Your legs act as a natural suspension system when you're riding, so keep your knees slightly bent to absorb jolts and help you land tricks. That way you won't be eating dirt when you ride over pavement cracks or roadkill. Relax your upper body and let your arms hang down ready to use for balance. Lean forwards and backwards on your trucks, crouch down and straighten your legs just to get used to your new skating life. Then wave at the neighbours staring at you over the garden fence. If that doesn't ruin your balance, it's time to move on.

Know when to stop

Hey, where're you going? **Oi, come back!** Before you push off, you'll need to know how to stop. Otherwise the next thing you know you'll end up in Alaska. Especially if you live at the top of a hill. To ensure you're back in time for tea, the easiest way to stop is to just jump off your board. But if you're travelling fast, your little cartoon legs won't be able to keep up with your body and you'll never see your expensive new board again. Like one of those horses that carry on to win the Grand National after they've thrown their rider, your board will cruise off into the sunset only to be run over by a passing car or snaffled by a tea leaf.

Instead, take your back foot off the board and drag it along the ground until you grind to a halt. After a few times your socks will start to show through your sneakers, so try the one-legged run, again with your back foot. But the best way to kill your speed and not your trainers is to make your board do all the work. Transfer your weight to your front foot, push the board through 90 degrees with your back foot and twist your shoulders so that you're facing forwards. Then push down evenly on all four wheels and you'll come to a screeching halt just outside the local newsagents like the pro you will be some day. You've just done a wheelslide. **Pop in and reward yourself with a can of coke.**

Now it's finally time to push off and shred some tarmac. Place your front foot over the front truck facing forwards and keep your weight there. Then put your back foot on the ground, level with your front leg, and give yourself a good push. Keep your knees bent and your pushing foot parallel and close to the board. Hey, you're moving! Give yourself another couple of pushes out of the kindness of your heart. When you've built up speed, lift your back foot up, place it on the tail and turn your feet sideways. As you get better, take bigger steps so that you go faster. Don't under any circumstances push with your front foot. Not only is it more difficult and less stable, but it'll make you a laughing stock and everyone down the skatepark will call you names, like mongo. Which is way, way worse than goofy.

Cruise control

So now you're rolling down the street with the wind in your hair. Life is good. But wait – what's that coming up in the distance? A manhole cover! You'd better learn to turn – and fast. Fortunately trucks make carving easy. If you're regular, lean backwards and push down on your heels and you'll turn left. This is called a frontside turn because your front is facing outwards. Turn right by leaning forwards and pushing down on your toes. This is a backside turn as your back is facing outwards. If you're goofy, you will turn in the opposite direction. Don't lean too far or the wheels will touch the deck (wheelbite) and throw you off. Practise without your board by standing straight and rocking forwards and backwards from your toes to your heels. Don't do it in public though, or men in white coats will cart you off to the funny farm. If it sounds complicated, don't worry. After a few goes on your new board, cruising will become as easy as falling off a log. Hmm, maybe that wasn't the right example to use. Oh well, you get the picture. Start off with your trucks quite tight and as you get better at carving, loosen them a little bit each day. Not until they fall off though. Otherwise you will too. Obviously.

chapter six
tricky Business

Over the next four chapters, **you'll learn how to do all manner of tricks**, starting with the easy ones and gradually getting harder. When learning a new trick, make your first few attempts on grass so that if you fall off, you don't end up with those "tweet tweet" things circling your head, like in cartoons. Then you can move on to concrete and learn on the move. It's harder than doing them stationary, but it will make life easier in the long run.

Practise in your driveway or in a public place before going to the skatepark, where you'll just get under everyone's feet (literally) and annoy all the more experienced riders, which is not a good start. When you do get to the skatepark and you see someone else pull off a sick trick, bang your skateboard on the coping to show your approval. Then these guys will be much more likely to help you. All the tricks in this book are explained as if you're regular-footed. But if you're goofy, just substitute left for right and clockwise for anti-clockwise.

Landing a trick once does not mean that you've mastered it and can move on. It was probably a fluke or as sketchy as you like. You have to keep practising until you can land it nine times out of ten. The more you do a trick, the better you get. Even famous pros like Tony Hawk are constantly learning. Remember that style and control can always be improved. Finally, if you're having problems with a particular trick, think it through carefully in your head. You'll be amazed how much this helps. Once you start dreaming in skateboard, you're there.

BASIC

These tricks may seem boring at first, but if you've got them down, clean and precise, then you'll have a head start when it comes to the more complicated stuff. Or come back here if you're having problems later on.

Manuals

Your good old-fashioned wheelie, but it's called a manual because on a skateboard you do it with no hands. Your front foot should be over the truck and your back foot on the kicktail. Get a little speed up, push down on the kicktail and release some of the weight on your front foot to lift up the nose so you're rolling on just your back wheels. You still have to push your front foot down a little to stay in control.

Make sure that the tail does not scrape the ground. Balance is the key and you may have to lean slightly backwards or forwards to get it slick. Hold the manual for as long as possible before bringing your front truck down.

Once you've got this, you can move on to the **spacewalk**, a trick nicked from aliens. It's basically a manual where you swing the nose from side to side. This moves you forward, in a circle or even backwards without pushing. Stand still and do a manual and push the nose 45 degrees to one side (think back to those boring maths lessons), swinging your arms in the opposite direction. This will stop you from turning further round and allow you to swing back in the other direction through to 45 degrees on the other side. Keep your weight above the back truck and don't let your tail scrape the ground. Carry on until you get cramp or you've lost three pounds, whichever comes first. And keep your swings as wide as your trousers.

The hardest manual trick is the **nose manual**, where you lift up the tail instead of the nose. Have your front foot on the nose and your back foot over the truck. While moving forward, transfer some of your weight to the front foot and push down on the nose, lifting up the tail. Keep some pressure on the back foot for balance. Hold it for as long as you can without the nose touching the ground, otherwise it'll be your own nose that's touching the ground. Learning this trick will help you with nollies later on.

Kickturns

A kick and turn – naturally. It's a faster way to change direction than carving and could get you out of a sticky situation if you're bombing head on towards a lamp post.

The humble kickturn cuts corners, if you will. If you can do a manual, kickturns should come easy. As soon as the front wheels start to come off the ground, pivot either towards your heels (frontside) or toes (backside). Keep your weight over the back foot and turn by twisting your hips and shoulders. At first just turn through a few degrees, then try to get up to 45 degrees and beyond.

Then you can move on to the **tic tac**. This is simply a series of kickturns in one direction and then the other. It's a good way to build up speed without pushing – so you can get a few more days' use out of your poor, battered Vans. Just kickturn to the right, then to the left and so on in quick succession. Tic tac is actually the name for the racket the board makes when you do this and *will have pedestrians diving for cover.*

As you get better, you can try an **old skool 180**. This is a kickturn through half a circle so you end up facing in the opposite direction. You'll need to wind your body up to give you momentum. To do a frontside 180, turn your hips to the right in preparation for the turn. Then, as you lift up the front wheels, quickly swivel your hips round to the left so you bring the nose down where your tail was. You'll find you're rolling backwards, which is known as riding fakie, a skill that'll come in very useful later on as you learn more complicated tricks.

The natural next step is to continue all the way round through a full circle so you end up in your original position. You'll need even more momentum from your hips for the **360**. Once you've done one, see how many you can do in a row. Make like you're in an old skool skating competition – back in the '60s before the ollie was invented, being able to pull off multiple kickturns was a sign of how good you were. They're still great for learning control.

Now it's time to **walk the dog**. No, not Fido – it's another trick. Walking the dog is a sequence of 180 kickturns pulled off with you facing the same direction – forwards – throughout. Place your front foot in the middle of the board facing straight ahead as you're rolling along. Then move your back foot up to the nose, press down lightly to lift up the tail and while still keeping your feet on the board, pull it round 180 degrees (if you're regular the board will turn clockwise) so that your back foot is behind you again. Always keep your front foot in the same place and the board will pivot underneath it. Believe me. Just keep moving the back foot up to the nose to push down and turn the board another 180 degrees. Turn the board smoothly otherwise you'll come off. Repeat until fade.

Jumps

Learning the **acid drop** is great practice for landing more complicated tricks. It's very simple. Holding your board in one hand, take a run up and then jump in the air. As you're off the ground, lift your knees towards your chest, put the deck underneath your feet, let go with your hand and straighten your legs to push the board down. Land the trick with your feet over the trucks. Get used to bending your knees to absorb the impact of landing. Your speed will make you roll away. When you get more confidence, try doing it off curbs, then one step, then a series of steps, then a mini-ramp until you can do it off really high objects. But maybe not the Empire State Building.

Another technique that will help you with landing is to

ride off an obstacle on to the ground. Again, start with curbs and slowly build up the height. Just cruise towards the drop at a reasonable speed and as you get to the edge, lean back on the tail slightly to lift the front wheels and let gravity do the rest. You need to be travelling fast enough for the tail to clear the object when you land. Practise coming down on all four wheels simultaneously and bend your knees on landing so that you ride away smoothly. Once you can do this, combine it with a manual – just ride it off the curb and land still on your back wheels.

Another very old skool trick is a jump while your board remains on the ground – let's call it the **high jump**. You'll have to set up a kind of obstacle course for this – at first try balancing a plank of wood on two piles of bricks. Ride your board up to it with both feet over the trucks and your weight nicely centred. Then jump up in the air and over the plank as your board goes underneath. You shouldn't need to jump forward as you are already travelling at the same speed and in the same direction as your board. Land cleanly with your feet over both trucks and roll off into the sunset. Next time put another brick under each pile to raise the height of the plank and try again – like doing the limbo but the other way round. If you make it up to 1.68m then you've broken the world record. Well done! Call Guinness.

"At first I found it difficult to learn new tricks but when you get something right and then practise it, the trick suddenly becomes a lot easier."
Robbie Tucket, 12, Ruislip

chapter seven
advanced tricks
- flat

Once you learn these, **you'll be a true street skater**. When you're trying to master the moves, be confident and you'll find it comes a lot easier. Learn at your own speed and don't try anything too complicated before you're ready or else you'll be eating hospital food for the next three weeks.

OLLIE

Ah, Mr Ollie. We've been expecting you. The ollie is the high priest of the skateboard trick kingdom. Once you get this down, you'll be flying. Literally. This is your first foray into the as-yet-uncharted world of "air". It's basically a jump where the board comes up with you. The secret's in the timing, which just takes endless practice. Be patient, it'll come eventually – poor old Alan "Ollie" Gelfard himself used to get his shoes and boards stolen by jealous skaters who thought he was using glue. These days, of course, you can use magnets, but that's another story (see Chapter 17).

How to do it

1. Have the "toe" of your back foot on the kicktail and your front foot in the middle of the board. You should be facing sideways. Have your weight centred and don't lean back. Crouch down so that your hands are nearly touching the ground like you're an orang utan.

2. Stamp down with your back foot and snap it back as you jump up in the air to get the board off the ground. Officially, the tail of the board should not actually touch the ground. Jump slightly forward and keep your shoulders in line with the board so that you stay directly above it.

3. The deck should be rising at 45 degrees. As it does, drag your front foot up the board towards the nose. This will help you get height and also level out your board. Tuck your legs up to your chest and the board will follow you.

4. When it's level, put your back foot back on and extend your legs to land on all four wheels with your feet over the trucks so that the board doesn't shoot out from underneath you. Keep your knees bent to absorb the impact on landing.

You want to be popping ollies, not your clogs. So practise on grass first. When you've got that down, you should learn to ollie while moving, so try it on concrete and land on grass, like going from your driveway to the front garden. Sorted? Now you can move on to the tarmac. Don't give up if you can't do it in a week. It can take some people, even pros, like, forever. Once you've got it sketchy, keep practising until you can do it with your eyes shut. Although that's not a recommendation. Then try to "float" in the middle of your ollie when you're in the air. Relax, lift your legs higher and try to spend longer off the ground. You'll find that your ollie gets longer and higher and you'll have more control and style. *You dude*.

Next try ollieing up a curb so that you know you've got air and to get the hang of the timing. Look at the curb as you approach it, then when you're about a metre away, look down at your board and just concentrate on doing the trick. You will sail over the curb as if it wasn't there. Then place drinks cans, skateboards, even dustbins in your way and ollie over them. Stairs are great for ollieing over and good for practising because you can start with one step and slowly move up until you're jumping five-sets and even ten-sets.

By now you should have realised that you can go anywhere you want. The world has become your skateboarding oyster.

Now if you've got your ollies down and you really want to look fly, try adding a few simple grabs. When you're floating through the air and the board's come up to do a meet and greet with your feet, reach down with your hand. You should already be in a crouching position with your knees tucked up to your chest so the board should be within touching distance. For a nose grab, hold on to the front of the board with your front hand, for a tail grab, lean back slightly and get a grip with your back hand. As you come to land, let go of the board. See Chapter 9 for some more complicated grabs. Then contact the local skate shop re sponsorship deals.

 ## TOP TIP

Your foot position will determine how much air you get. The further back your front foot, the higher you will go but the trick will be more difficult to control. Therefore at first it'll probably be easier to have your front foot just behind the front bolts. This will allow you to pop over a small curb and stay on the board. As you get better, move your foot further back. Also the quicker you pop and the higher you drag your front foot up the board, the higher you will ollie. If you're falling off when you land it's due to your weight distribution. If your front foot comes off the right of the board, for example, you are leaning too much to that side. So adjust your foot position or launch angle a little to the left. The same goes if you're falling off the front or back.

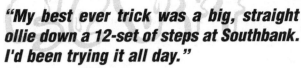

> **"My best ever trick was a big, straight ollie down a 12-set of steps at Southbank. I'd been trying it all day."**
> Scott Fraser, 30, Northamptonshire

180 OLLIES

Like most tricks you're going to learn from now on, these can be done frontside or backside. It's an ollie with a 180-degree turn in mid-air so you'll have to be comfortable riding backwards because you're going to land and roll away fakie.

How to do it

If you've perfected your 180 kickturns, this trick will come a lot easier. Do everything the same as for an ollie but as you prepare for take-off, wind up your body a little in the opposite direction to the way you're going to spin. This builds up momentum for the turn. The faster you go, the easier it will be to rotate. Pop the ollie as normal but as you do, twist your shoulders and throw your arms round as you unwind to the left for a frontside 180 ollie. Your body should take you round at least 90 degrees and your legs will follow but you'll have to push through the rest of the turn with your back leg. As you ollie, drag your front foot to just past the front bolts so that you can easily adjust your board position when you land if you're not straight. Keep

your balance. Your board should be directly underneath you the whole time as you guide it round with your feet to land above the trucks. If you're not comfortable riding away fakie (you've been skiving skate class again, haven't you?), then do a 180 kickturn as you land to get you back to where you started. If you're going to pop a gigantic ollie – and it is easier the higher you go – remember to rotate slower as you'll be in the air for longer. You show-off. Now do it backside. It's a little harder because you can't see where you're going. That'll learn yer!

If you're having trouble spinning all the way through 180, land on the back wheels and pivot the rest of the turn with the front of the board in the air. You might also find it easier to nail the frontside if you have your front foot slightly hanging over the heel side of the board so it doesn't slip in the spin. Also try putting your front foot slightly further forward than with a normal ollie to keep more control.

"I love the amount of tricks you can do. I've just done a 180 – it felt brilliant!"
Tom Duggan, 14, Croydon

"I started skateboarding because I thought it would be a challenge, something I could get good at. When I did a 360 ollie, I was like, 'Yes, finally!' It took me about a month."
Chris Kovacs, 13, Aylesbury

NOLLIE

The nollie is an ollie off the nose of your board. Hence "n" for nollie.

How to do it

This is an ollie except with your feet in reverse. So your front foot should be on the nose and your back foot just in front of the truck. Pop the nose and push forwards a little as you jump up. Drag your back foot down the board to get the height, and level out the board underneath you as you tuck your legs up. Then extend your legs and land with your feet over the trucks. The nollie is much harder than the ollie and feels unnatural at first. You'll need to build up enough speed so that you don't stop when you pop the nose otherwise you and your board will be going nowhere. Except to Casualty.

TOP TIP

If you're having trouble with nollies, it might be easier to do the fakie ollie (which isn't a nollie). Although you're riding backwards, a fakie ollie is still performed in your natural stance. A nollie is technically switchstance.

POP SHOVIT

An ollie where the board spins 180 degrees underneath you so you land fakie. Unless you're really flash and spin it a full circle like Matt Hensley used to do over bins. Also check out Donny Barley and Matt Rodriguez for some pro tips. Backside is usually easier than frontside. The Pop Shovit is pretty simple and looks good but it's been a bit neglected of late so show it some love.

How to do it

You can practise turning your board when you're not even on it. Stand still with just your back foot on the tail. Push down and pull your back foot back towards the heel, then catch the board with the same foot on the nose after it spins round 180 degrees. Now climb on and place your feet as for an ollie but make sure your back foot is right in the centre of the tail as you take off, otherwise the board will flip as it turns. To do a backside 180, kick your back foot towards the heel straight after you've popped the board. It will turn clockwise underneath you. Watch the board closely so you can stop it turning by landing on it in mid-air with your front foot. You'll need to ollie quite high so that the board has more space to turn. For the frontside version, put your back foot closer to the heel edge and kick your leg out forwards. The board turns anti-clockwise. The 180 is

actually quite a slow spin, so don't kick too hard. To do a 360, just give it a bigger shove and get more height to give the board time to spin.

 TOP TIP

Your board might be turning but you don't want to. So keep above it at all times otherwise you'll miss the landing. When you're learning, don't pop as hard as you would for an ollie and the board will spin slower so it's easier to catch.

KICKFLIP

An ollie where the board flips horizontally through a full circle underneath you as you jump. If you're regular, the board turns anti-clockwise, if you're goofy it flips clockwise. Rodney Mullen was the first to do it and Tom

Penny probably got them down the smoothest so watch one of his videos (see Chapter 18). They're not easy but once you pull one off, you'll be too stoked for words.

How to do it

1. You're best off practising the basic motion of a kickflip from a sitting position. Take a seat on a park bench with just your back foot on the tail. Pop the tail and as the board comes up in the air, give it a flick on the heel side with your front foot near the nose. Watch it flip and then catch it on the ground with your back foot.

2. Now climb on. Place your front foot at a 45-degree angle just behind the truck with your heel hanging off the edge of the board. Your back foot should be almost square on right on the tail and you should feel like you're on your toes. The further back your back foot is, the higher the board will rise, but you will be less stable. Your shoulders should be parallel to the board. This position might feel a bit odd and could make you start veering off at an angle, but you'll get used to it.

3. Compress your body as you prepare to jump up and pop the board as you would for an ollie. Keeping your front foot straight, lightly drag it up (the higher you drag, the higher the board will pop) and off the heel side of the board just before it reaches the nose. As your front foot comes off, give the board a flick with your toes using your ankle. Kick your foot out sideways so that the board doesn't hit it as it flips. The faster you flick, the faster your board will flip. Don't kick down or too far out otherwise you won't be able to get your foot back underneath you in time to land the trick. Your back foot should also come off the board. Try to jump straight up in the air and stay parallel to the board.

4. Tuck both legs right up to your chest to give the board time and space to flip and stay directly over it (you might have to jump forwards a little). Always keep your eyes on the board. As soon as you see the griptape, slam your feet back down on to the board directly over the trucks and push it back down to the ground. Bend your knees when you land. Try to concentrate on getting both your feet back on the board rather than spinning it. It's better to land an upside-down board than not at all. If this is happening a lot, then you either need to flick a bit harder or jump higher.

5. Read these instructions three times, memorise them, then try not to think too much about all the things you have to do, have confidence and the trick will come naturally. After about six months.

TOP TIP

Foot placement is a very personal thing, like nasal hair. You might want to have your front foot slightly further back, in between the two trucks, but then you'll probably find it harder to get out of the way when your board flips. So experiment, experiment, experiment. If you keep landing with your front foot on the ground, lean forward more as you jump and really commit to the trick. Try practising on grass next to a park bench. Do the trick and pull yourself up with the bench. Then land that baby. Now try it with just one hand. Then land it again. Now get back on the concrete where you belong. If kickflips are still giving you a migraine, try the heelflip first. A lot of people find them easier. The weirdos.

"The first real kickflip I made was in my driveway in 1983, totally stationary. I'd try it for two hours and maybe make five. Two weeks later, I could move a little. I remember being really stoked because it was a new thing and I called it a magic flip. The name obviously didn't stick."

Rodney Mullen, pro skater

"The best thing is when you land a trick you've been trying for ages. The kickflip took me about four weeks but when I did it, it felt really good."

Craig Stewart, 13, Streatham, London

"The secret is to keep trying and don't give up. Patience and a positive attitude also help. Skating is supposed to be fun. Don't criticise other skaters and remember you were a beginner once too!"

Steve Caballero, pro skater

HEELFLIP

Also invented by Lord Mullen, the heelflip is almost exactly the same as the kickflip except the board flips in the opposite direction.

How to do it

Set up the same as for the kickflip except your front foot should be towards the toe edge with the heel of your back foot just hanging off the board. Some people like to have their front toes hanging off the board. When you pop the board, drag your front foot up and diagonally off the toe side of the board just before the nose. To make it spin, you don't so much flick it with your heel, more roll the whole side of your foot as it leaves the board. Kick your front foot out forwards and slightly to the side so that it's out of the way. Tuck both legs up to your chest. Bring your feet back over the board and down on to it when you see the griptape. Land and high-five your mates.

TOP TIP

You might find this easier if you start with your feet in the classic ollie position as it makes the board spin faster. Also try looking at the part of the board you want to "kick" as you do the trick.

Think you're a bit tasty now? Go back and relearn all these tricks in switchstance. Then combine the pop shovit with a kickflip (varial kickflip) and heelflip (varial heelflip). Now do *them* switch. Only now you can start bragging.

> *"Once you learn how to ollie, the rest comes quite easily. Recently I've been practising a varial kickflip. It took me three weeks. I was very happy as I've only been learning for seven months."*
> Vlad Vassil, 15, Russia

chapter eight
Born Slappy

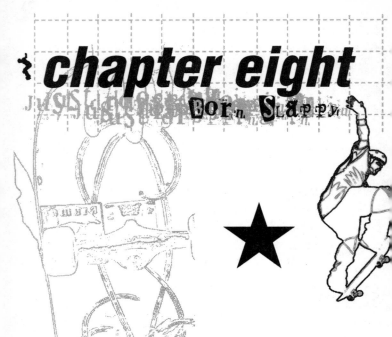

Life's such a grind when you're a skateboarder. But that's a good thing. Grinds and slides are when you ride over an obstacle with a part of your board that isn't your wheels – if it's the trucks it's a grind, the deck and it's a slide. Both produce a great screeching noise that makes all the pigeons fly away whether you do them backside or frontside. Backside is when you approach the obstacle with your heels facing it and frontside is when your toes are closest. Grinds and slides open up a whole new dimension of skateboarding because once you've got these tricks up your sleeve, you'll be able to use any part of your board to pull off sick moves.

GRINDS

Normally done on rails as you need a straight, flat surface that's thin enough to fit between your trucks. Watch out though, grinds are very fast. Practise on low objects first, like curbs, then move up to grind rails and fun boxes. The grinds below are equally easy (or difficult!) frontside or backside, so just start off skating the way you personally feel most comfortable. When you're learning, approach the obstacle from a parallel direction. As you improve, come in at more of a slant, getting up to 30 or 45 degrees. It'll look way better and older kids will start offering you lifts to skateparks.

SLAPPY

Practise grinds before you can ollie on low obstacles such as curbs.

How to do it

Approach frontside from around 30 degrees, with your feet over both trucks and rolling quite fast. This will allow you to climb the curb without jumping. Just before you reach it, take the weight off your front foot and use your speed to ride up over it. Transfer your weight to the front and the back trucks will follow. The edge of the curb should be between your front and back trucks. Stay perfectly balanced with your weight directly over the middle of the board to 50-50 grind until you start losing momentum. To come off, put your weight over the back truck so that you can lift the front wheels off. Transfer your weight forward and you will peel off. Congratulations, you've just nailed your first grind. Now do it backside.

The slappy will help you no end when it comes to more difficult grinds. And although it's not the most complicated trick, it'll still impress your gran. So practise and practise until you can do it backwards. Or fakie. Oh, that is backwards.

> **"Some days I can hardly slappy a curb. Skating is a mental battle more than a physical one, a battle with yourself."**
> *Matt Mumford, pro skater*

50-50

The slappy is a 50-50 because you use both front and back trucks to grind. Now you're going to learn how to ollie into them.

How to do it

The height of your jump is crucial – too low and you won't make the trick, too high and you'll find it difficult to land on the obstacle. Practise on low stuff like curbs. Approach frontside, riding parallel to the obstacle. Get some speed up and pop your ollie when you're close. If you can't get both trucks to land at the same time, come down on your back truck first and then drop the front down. Keep your knees bent so you can adjust your balance. The hardest thing is getting on. Once you are, you should stay there.

On a rail, start your grind near the end so you don't have so far to travel and slowly build up to longer ones. If you're running out of speed and want to come off before the end, dismount with a kickturn. Press down on the kicktail to lift the front truck up and then transfer your weight to the front, level out the board as you come off and make sure both feet are over the trucks. Stretch your legs but get ready to bend your knees to absorb the landing.

As you improve, approach from gradually wider angles and ollie sideways. Drag the board in the right direction with your front foot. You should be parallel to the obstacle with your board level and directly underneath you when you land, otherwise you'll bail. Now try it backside. Your work here is done.

TOP TIP

If you're grinding on a wide obstacle like a curb which is too large to fit between your trucks, lock your heel-side wheels against the edge and press down on your toes.

5-0

The "Hawaii" 5-0 is a combination of the 50-50 and the manual, so you're grinding on just your back truck.

How to do it

Get the knack of the 5-0 by perfecting your ollie to manual on the flat. Instead of coming down on all four wheels, land on just the back two by keeping your back foot over the tail and your weight over the back truck. Your nose will remain in the air like you're a stuck-up rich boy.

Now repeat over your chosen obstacle. You'll need to lean slightly further forward as you grind to pick up more momentum. If it makes it easier to balance, try dragging the tail along the obstacle too, although this will slow you down and you won't be able to grind as far. Learn by trial and error how much weight to put on your back truck and how much on the front – remember, you still need some pressure on the nose, otherwise you'll fly off backwards.

Come out by leaning down on the front to convert to a 50-50 or by turning your board and shoulders to ride the manual off the side. Either transfer your weight back to the middle of the board to level it out or continue the manual and land on your back truck. Ride it cowboy. **Yeeee-ha!**

 TOP TIP

If you're having trouble, try doing it from a stationary position at first, ollieing onto the obstacle and just holding the manual. Once you've got that down four times out of five, go away and listen to your favourite skate CD on full volume and don't think about the trick. Then come back, push like the wind and just go for it.

> **"When you try a trick for a while and then you finally land it, you get a real adrenaline rush. You start getting really obsessed."**
>
> Charles Nicholson, 13, Balham, London

NOSE GRIND

You're really going to have to get your nose to the, er, grindstone for this one. A nose grind is performed on just your front truck with your tail in the air, like a nose manual. As you might imagine, it's the grind that's most likely to end in a world of hurt because if you get it wrong, your face will become best friends with Mr T.A.R. McAdam.

How to do it

The secret to landing this is in your front leg. You'll also need to build up a head of steam. As you ollie, keep dragging that front foot up the board past the usual point and continue on to the nose. This will push

the nose down and the tail up and allow you to transfer most of your weight on to the front foot as you land. Straighten your front leg and drive the truck down on to the obstacle but try not to let the nose touch.

As with the 5-0, weight distribution is crucial to your balance so lean forward but remember to keep some pressure on your back foot to hold the position. But don't lean too far forward otherwise you'll just grind to a stop. You need to kind of push the board through this trick with your front foot. Keep your trucks parallel to the obstacle.

Coming off is a whole lot more difficult. You're going to have to pull a mini nollie, so snap down with your front foot and drag your back foot towards the tail to level the board out. Make sure you haven't lost so much speed in your grind that your tail bashes the obstacle as you dismount. Extend your legs and get ready to bend your knees when you land. Then ride off in the direction of prospective sponsors.

 TOP TIP

Now you can move on to crooked grinds, smith grinds and salad grinds. Just make sure you avoid the nine-to-five grind for as long as is humanly possible. Skateboarding isn't very popular in offices.

"If you're scared of a trick and you start thinking about what you're doing, it's going to get you more scared. I picture myself rolling away from the thing before I even hit it."

Danny Way, pro skater

SLIDE RULES

If you know how to stall, ie to land on an object, transfer your weight on to it and hold your position before dropping off – then slides will come much easier. You'll also need to have your ollies well and truly sussed because the height you jump is all-important. Too low and you won't make the trick, too high and you'll overshoot.

Most slides are done on curbs or ledges. These are generally a lot less smooth than rails so the added friction will slow you down and make sliding harder. If you can't find anything with a piece of metal along the side, smear some wax all over the obstacle (don't use too much or you'll lose the board from beneath your feet) and get some serious speed up. You can either use a plain old candle, or buy some specialist stuff from a skate shop.

Start by approaching at an angle, anywhere from 30 to 45 degrees, to make it easier to turn on to the obstacle. If you find your board is hitting the obstacle before you land on it, start to ollie a little further away. When your 180 ollies are down to a tee, you can ride up parallel. The extra speed generated will make you slide further and your mates' jaws drop lower. Also the faster you go, the longer you'll keep your balance.

You'll have to try each slide a number of times before you work out the body and feet position that feels right for you. Lean back slightly if you're sticking, lean forwards if you're toppling over backwards. Keep your legs bent and extend your arms for balance to help you stay on.

BACKSIDE BOARDSLIDE

This is a slide on the middle of your board between your two trucks. Unlike the other slides, it's better suited to rails or double-sided ledges as control comes easier if your feet are nicely balanced over the trucks on either side of the obstacle. Try your first one on as wide a rail as possible to give you more support or start off on a curb. You won't slide very far but it's a good way to learn. Then if you slam, the only thing you'll injure will be your pride.

How to do it

As with 180 ollies, wind up your body in preparation for turning when you lift off. Then ollie, unwind and turn the board so it's perpendicular to the obstacle (at 90 degrees). Guide the deck with your front foot so that your feet and body are facing forwards. Remember to get enough height for your front wheels to clear the obstacle. As you're turning, make sure you stay vertical and directly over the board. Land with your feet just outside the trucks and your weight slightly forward but spread evenly between your two feet as you balance on your heels. Hold the slide for as long as possible. ***You're king of the world!***

It's easiest to come off at the end of the obstacle. Take some weight off your front foot, lean back a bit and twist your shoulders and hips to turn the board. If there is no end in sight or you're running out of steam, look over your back shoulder, twist your body and lift your front foot to get the nose back over the obstacle. Continue turning as you centre your weight to bring the board level, straighten your legs and bend your knees as you land with both feet over the trucks. All you need now is a crowd of admirers.

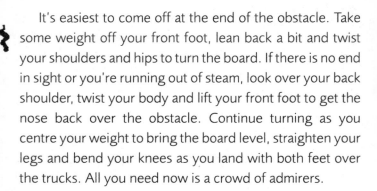

TOP TIP

If your back leg is trailing when you're sliding, try approaching the obstacle from a slightly wider angle.

FRONTSIDE BOARDSLIDE

Way more tricky because you can't see where the hell you're going. So you imagine it's straight to hospital. And, as every skater knows, once you've lost the battle in your mind, the next thing you'll lose is one of your limbs. The secret is to keep your upper body parallel to the obstacle while your lower half remains perpendicular. Then you can look over your shoulder. To come off at the end, just unwind your lower body back in line with your top half. Job done.

BACKSIDE NOSESLIDE

As you might have guessed, this is when you slide on the nose of your board, with the front truck nestling up to the edge so you're perpendicular to the obstacle. It's best to do these on curbs and ledges. Some people find this easier than the boardslide because you don't have to get your front trucks over the obstacle before you start sliding.

How to do it

Place your front foot just behind the front bolts and do half a 180 ollie so you're facing forwards. Drag your foot up to land with all your weight on the nose and keep your board level. Lean forward on the nose to slide. At first, it's easiest to come off fakie – just swivel your hips and shoulders. Once you've got this off pat, dismount the proper way with a mini nollie. Pop the nose of your board and guide it round and off the obstacle, using your front foot. Bend your legs and lean forward as you land with both feet over the trucks so the board doesn't shoot out from underneath you.

FRONTSIDE NOSESLIDE

Like the frontside boardslide, this is much more difficult because you're sliding backwards. So remember to keep your shoulders parallel to the obstacle and your lower body perpendicular so you can come off by unwinding your lower body back in line with your top half and guiding the board round with your front foot.

TOP TIP

To land it fakie, slide with your whole body perpendicular, look over your back shoulder and allow your momentum to carry you round.

⚡ TAILSLIDES

A frontside tailslide is very similar to a backside noseslide, it's just that to get on to the obstacle you ollie 90 degrees in the opposite direction to land with all your weight on the tail. You'll probably find it harder getting up on to the obstacle but easier getting off it – you just lean forward a little and turn out. If you're doing it backside, keep your whole body perpendicular to the obstacle. Then, when you want to come off, just turn your shoulders and the nose of the board forward. Ride off into the sunset because here endeth this lesson.

> **"It made me feel great when I first did a tailslide, especially as everyone clapped me on."**
> *Luke Pody, 15, Billingshurst*

LUKE

chapter nine
ramp tricks

Once you move on to ramps, even mini ones, you really need to wear safety gear. **You'll be skating faster and higher** than you've been used to, so when you make the trip to the skatepark, make sure you've packed a helmet, elbow pads, wrist guards and – most important of all – kneepads. Then when you realise you can't make a trick you can come off your board without risk of serious injury (see Chapter 4 for how to bail). And don't just put them in your Eastpak to keep your mum happy. Take them out and put them on when you arrive. Otherwise you'll be kicking yourself when you wake up in a hospital bed. That's if you can still move your legs.

Most skateparks have ramps of all different sizes. You should start on the smallest halfpipe you can find and gradually move up when you're confident enough. Mini-ramps have no vert (short for vertical) section and go up to about six feet high. The average vert ramp is 11 feet high and 30 feet wide. Before you get on a ramp for the first time, you should know the basics – at the very least how to stop, kickturn and skate fakie.

Start on the flat at the bottom of a halfpipe and push up one side with your feet over the trucks. As you get better, move your back foot towards the tail. When you're learning, don't use any angles – always skate straight up and down. Don't worry about making it to the top (the lip) at first. When you run out of steam, just use the slope to roll down fakie and back up the other side.

Now you need to start pumping to get more height. This is the same principle as your kid brother or sister uses to get higher on the swings in the playground. So if they can do it . . . Bend your legs and crouch down as you approach the side of the ramp. When you reach the transition (the curve between the vertical and horizontal sections), extend your legs to push down on your board and throw your upper body in the direction you're travelling. As you get higher, gradually crouch down again. Transfer your weight to your back foot to come back down. Look round behind you in the direction you're travelling. Straighten your legs and push down again through the transition. Then repeat on the opposite side, staying over the board at all times. It will feel weird at first when you're pumping fakie, but you'll soon get the hang of it. Try using your arms to help you with the timing – swing them up as you climb the ramp and back again as you come down. As you get better, you'll climb higher until you reach the top. Then you can start to pull some tricks.

Alternatively, instead of coming down fakie, do a 180 kickturn. Backside is easiest to learn first. Start turning your shoulders in the direction you want to go as you're riding up, then when you reach the peak of your climb, press down on the kicktail to lift up the front wheels. Turn your shoulders and head through 180 degrees and your lower body will follow. Land your front wheels and lean forward to come down. Don't put too much weight on the back foot otherwise you'll spin round too far. Practise so you can do it nice and smooth – a 180 turn is not as big a rotation as it seems, so take your time, keep control and you'll come back down in a straight line. Pro skater Steve Caballero once did continuous 180 kickturns for over an hour on a ramp in Sweden. See if you can get anywhere close.

DROPPING IN

After your first couple of sessions on the halfpipe, you'll be bored starting at the bottom every time. So you'll want to drop in. Word of warning, though – this is far more dangerous than just popping round to see your mates. It's a different kind of dropping in altogether.

How to do it

Start with the smallest ramp you can find. Stand on the tail with your back foot and position it so that the back wheels are just over the edge, nestling against the coping. Then step out and place your front foot over the front truck. Transfer your weight forwards as you push down so the front wheels slam on to the ramp. Crouch over the board and keep leaning slightly forwards with your shoulders and hips parallel and your weight centred. Keep looking forward. Some people find that it helps to reach towards the nose with the front hand. As you get to the transition, even out your weight. You have to execute this trick with supreme confidence because if you get The Fear, you'll lean backwards, your board will shoot out from underneath you and you'll have to pray to the gods of skateboarding that you can bail better than you can drop in.

NOSE STALL

This is when you balance with the nose of the board on the lip of the ramp. With your front foot over the truck, ride up the ramp and when you get to the top, transfer your weight to the front foot and slide it on to the nose. Press down so that it's flat on the lip with your front wheels against the edge and your back wheels in the air. Ideally the board should be level. Hold the position for as long as you can before transferring your weight back over the centre of the board. Your back wheels will come back down on to the ramp. Bend your knees, stay centred over the board and lean slightly down the slope to roll back to the bottom.

FAKIE TAIL STALL

Opposite of a nose stall. Be flash and do it straight afterwards on the opposite wall. With your back foot over the truck, ride up the ramp fakie and when you get to the top, transfer your weight to the back foot and slide it on to the tail. Press down so that it's flat on the lip with your back wheels against the edge and your front wheels up in the air. Hold it. Then drop back in as if you're, er, dropping in.

ROCK TO FAKIE

For this trick you briefly balance on the coping with the middle of your board (similar to a boardslide), then drop back in. As you ride up the ramp, your back foot should be on the tail and your front foot just behind the truck. Overshoot slightly and push down on the kicktail so that your front truck clears the top of the ramp. Then push down with your front foot so that your front wheels touch the lip and rock the board on the coping. Hold the position with your back wheels in the air. Transfer your weight to your back foot as you rock back and use the tail to lift your front wheels over the coping. Watch them like a Tony Hawk because if they hang up, it'll send you flying backwards and headfirst into an early bath. With lots of Radox. Put your front wheels down and ride away fakie.

ROCK AND ROLL

Similar to the rock to fakie except you roll back down regular after a 180-degree kickturn at the top of the ramp. Roll up to the top and rest your front wheels on the lip as above. Then lean back into the ramp, put your back wheels on the surface and start twisting your shoulders and hips to do a backside turn. As you push down on the tail to lift your front wheels up and over the coping, guide your board through a 180 pivot with your front foot. Bend your knees as you land the front wheels and remember to throw your weight forward as you do when you drop in. Once you've got this down, try it frontside.

MIXING IT UP

Once you're confident with these tricks, incorporate moves you learnt on the flat as well as grinds and slides. When you get to the top of the ramp, ollie or kickturn into a 50-50 grind or a 5-0 along the coping. Ride diagonally across the ramp to get the angle to pull off lipslides. Learn them frontside and backside. Build up your speed so that you can get some air. Then flip backside 180 ollies over the top of the ramp. Now you're the boss. Pack your bags and join the circus.

"If I make a trick, then cool, and if not, I don't get mad. For the helicopter jump I looked at it as a fantasy, like, 'Whoa, is that possible?' Afterwards I sat back and thought, 'That was crazy, I didn't hesitate to do that.'"

Danny Way, pro skater

GRABS

The best place to learn grabs is off that launch ramp you built in your back yard. When you're in the air, crouch down as low as possible to reach the board with your hands. Remember to let go before you land otherwise you'll either make mincemeat of your fingers or do your back in. And then you'll have to walk round bent double like your granddad. Which is so not a good look. Once you've got to know them, introduce your new grab friends to the ramps in the skatepark as you fly over gaps and stairs. Despite having bizarre names, all grabs are cool and will become some of your best buddies. Get to know as many as you can.

Nose grab: Front hand on nose

Tail grab: Back hand on tail

Mute grab: Front hand on middle of board on toe edge

Indy grab: Back hand on middle of board on toe edge

Melon grab: Front hand on middle of board on heel edge

Stalefish grab: Back hand on middle of board on heel edge

Roastbeef grab: Back hand through legs to middle of board on heel edge

SKATING THE WEB

http://www.bobstricktips.com Want to do more complicated tricks? Bob's your uncle.

http://www.geocities.com/Colosseum/Loge/7982/trick.html How-to guide to the basics with easy-to-download video clips.

http://www.girlsskatebetter.com/trick_tips.html Basic and advanced tricks with photo sequences.

http://www.skatersinc.com Loads of video clips.

http://www.spg540.tripod.com/trickn.html Comprehensive list with simple, easy-to-follow explanations.

> **"Skateboarding is hard and everyone learns at their own pace. Don't get caught up in what's cool, what's not, or what tricks you should learn. Do whatever makes you happy."**
>
> *Andy MacDonald, pro skater*

chapter ten

skateparks, spots and events

There are now more skateparks in the UK than ever before as local councils have finally cottoned on to the fact that skateboarding is here to stay. **Duh, keep up,** Councillor! Some of the outdoor concrete parks have been around since the '70s, while newer indoor ones are being built all the time – the only plus point about having such lame weather is that we have more indoor parks than most other European countries. Overleaf is a list of major skateparks around the British Isles. Outdoor parks have ramps and features like snake runs (a twisty downhill course) and moguls (little bumps) and even bowls. Indoor parks are normally built of wood, designed by boarders and have funboxes, pyramids, grind rails and all kinds of ramps. They often have a skate shop attached and hold competitions for all ages and levels. This is where to go in winter. Check out the Crossfire Riot Bus service for transport to the larger indoor parks. You get to travel with pro riders, watch skate videos en route and listen to good tuneage – call 07798 855216 or check out www.crossfirenight.com. Try to visit skateparks away from peak times like holidays and weekends when they're quieter. That way other skaters won't get under your feet the whole time. Unless you're really good of course – then you can just ollie over them.

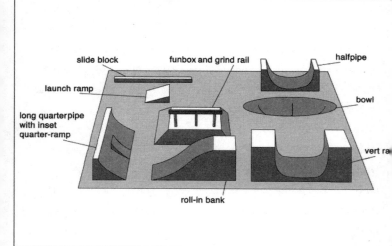

NORTH

Blackburn *Rhythm Skatepark*, Unit 29, Gillibrand Mill, Percival Street, Darwen, 01254 721117 (indoor)

Blackpool *Ramp City WSA*, Cropper Road, Marton, 01253 699005, www.rampcitywsa.co.uk (indoor) All manner of ramps, quarterpipes and rails

Bolton *Bones II Skatepark*, Gilnow Lane, Deane, 01204 392939, www.bonesskatepark.com (indoor) Large well-designed street course including ramps, boxes, spines and rails, plus cool gear from local shop

Chester *The Bone Yard*, Tattenhall Works, Tattenhall Road, 01829 770771 (indoor)

Chesterfield *Unit 1 Skatepark*, Lockford Lane, 01246 231133 (indoor)

Cleveland *R-Kade*, Majuba Road, Redcar, 01642 483520, www.r-kadeskatepark.com (indoor)

Dewsbury *Aggro Verts*, Unit 54, Calderwharf Mills, Huddersfield Road, 01924 439439, www.aggroverts.co.uk (indoor) Split-level street course with a 50-foot mini-ramp

Doncaster *Great Northern Youth Centre*, Great North Road, Woodlands, 01302 723531 (indoor) Wooden ramps for 13–19-year-olds

Grimsby *The Krem*, Convamore Road, off Ladysmith Road, 01472 359093 (indoor)

Liverpool *Rampworx 2*, 1–3 Leckwith Road, Netherton, 0151 530 1500, www.rampworx2.co.uk (indoor) Sprawling street course, vert ramps, spine ramps, jump boxes and a gigantic bowl. Plus a foam pit so you can practise ultra-gnarly stunts without knocking your head off

Manchester *Woodhouse Skatepark*, Unit 1, Victoria Industrial Estate, Pollard Street, Ancoates, www.woodhouseskatepark.co.uk (indoor)

Pocklington *Monty's Skatepark*, Bilby Lane, www.monty's-skatepark.co.uk (outdoor)

Preston *The Grind Project*, Southgate Mill, Southgate, 01772 828284, www.grind.co.uk (indoor) Huge indoor set-up with much grinding opportunity

Sheffield *Devonshire Green Skatepark*, Devonshire Street, 0114 275 7143 (outdoor, free)

Sheffield *The House Skatepark*, Bardwell Road, Neepsend, 0114 249 0055 (indoor) Massive street course and no BMX boys allowed. Yay!

Stockport *Bones Skatepark*, Canal Street, 0161 480 8118, www.bones-skatepark.co.uk (indoor) With all the mod-cons, a separate beginners' section and gear from Note

Stockton-On-Tees *APE Skate*, Martinet Road, Thornaby,

www.ape-skate.com, 01642 764114 (indoor)

Sunderland *Vertx Skatepark*, 76 Toward Road, Hendon, 0191 514 0514, www.sunderlandskatepark.com (indoor) Wooden paradise with gnarly vert ramp

Whitley Bay *Skate City*, The Promenade (inside Fun City), 0191 253 1571, www.skatecity.4t.com (indoor) Small but perfectly formed

> ## "The best skatepark I've been to is Rampworx in Liverpool. It's massive. They've got a real nice bowl with extensions and bowled out corners, driveways, spine ramps, vert ramps, everything. It's brilliant."

Harry Bray, 15, Vans Grom

MIDLANDS

Bedworth *Bedworth Street Complex*, behind Bedworth Leisure Centre, Miners Welfare Park, Coventry Road, Warwickshire, www.nuneatonandbedworthskateparks.com (outdoor, free) Big new street course with floodlights

Birmingham *Epic*, The Old Bus Depot, 582 Moseley Road, Moseley, 07961 071920 (indoor) Recently opened Epic is exactly that. Two separate street areas, a 6-foot bowl and a 14-foot vert ramp. Plus all mod-cons like shower blocks, café, video screen, in-house radio station and BMX trails

Birmingham *Wheels*, 1a Adderley Road South, Saltley, 0121 771 0725 (outdoor, free)

Derby *Storm*, Colombo Street, 01332 201768 (indoor)

Kidderminster *Roll'N'Ride*, Stadium Close, 01562 747040 (indoor)

Leicester *Edge Skatepark*, Unit 5, Thames Street,

www.edgeskatepark.com (indoor) New park with bowl, mini-ramp, vert wall and street course

Northampton *Radlands*, Studland Road, Kingsthorpe Industrial Estate, 01604 792060, www.radlands.com (indoor) Eleven years ago, this was the first indoor skatepark in Europe. Hosted the Brit championships through most of the late '90s. Check out the graffiti and Wednesday's "pro" nights

Oxford *Meadow Lane Park*, junction of Meadow Lane and Jackdaw Lane (outdoor, free)

Peterborough *Y2SK8 Towermead Industrial Estate*, Fletton High Street, 01733 358228 (indoor) Everything you'll ever need

Redditch *Redditch Skatepark*, Icknield Drive, Arrow Head Park, Matchborough, 01527 524550 (outdoor)

Shrewsbury *Shrewsbury Skatepark*, Monkmoor Recreational Park, Racecourse Avenue, 01743 361088 (outdoor)

Telford Sk8mental, Unit B, Stafford Park, 01952 299558, www.sk8mental.co.uk

Walsall *WS2 Skatepark*, Wolverhampton Street, ws2.sytes.net (indoor)

Wolverhampton *Warped Skatepark*, Unit 7, Parkside Industrial Estate, Hickman Avenue, 01902 453634, www.warpedsports.com (indoor) Sick street course with wall rides, grind bars and vert ramp

Worcester *RampAge Skatepark*, 13 Orchard Street, 01905 359660, www.rampageuk.com (indoor) Brand new

SOUTH

Barnstaple *Skate Rock Park*, Newport, North Devon, 01271 372027, www.skaterockpark.co.uk (outdoor)

Beckenham *Harvington Skatepark*, PABYA Centre, 56 Churchfield Road, Kent, 020 8658 9663 (indoor)

Bournemouth *Slades Farm*, Slades Farm Road (outdoor, free)

Bracknell *Longhill Skatepark*, Harvest Ride, Winkfield (outdoor, free)

Bridport *The Trick Factory*, Industrial Estate behind police station, 0117

907 9995 (indoor)

Brighton *The Level*, Lewes Road (outdoor)

Bristol *Sk8 & Ride*, 74 Avon Street, 0117 907 9995 (indoor)

Bristol *Bedminster*, Dean Lane, Bedminster (outdoor, free)

Bristol *Hengrove Skatepark*, Hengrove Leisure Complex (outdoor)
Concrete paradise served up in a nice bowl

Broadstairs *Revolution*, Oakwood Industrial Estate, Dane Valley Road,
01843 866707, www.revolutionskatepark.co.uk (indoor) Mini-ramps,
wall rides, fun boxes, quarterpipes, spine and corner bowl

Caterham *Skaterham*, The Chapel, at the entrance to the old army
barracks, Surrey, 01883 348557, www.skaterham.com (indoor) It's true,
skating is a religion! Skate inside its first church

Crawley *Crawley Skatepark*, Crawley Leisure Centre, 07885 213285
(indoor & outdoor, free)

Croydon *Croydon Skatepark*, Wandle Park, Cornwall Road (outdoor,
free) New, £60,000 all-metal playground

Farnborough *Farnborough Skatepark*, next to Farnborough Recreation
Centre, Westmead (outdoor, free) Mix of wood, steel and Skatelite and
floodlit until 10pm

Great Yarmouth *The Park*, Main Cross Road, 01493 853322,
www.theparkwarehouse.co.uk (indoor) A year old and described as
"the best in the country" by *Sidewalk* magazine

Harrow *Harrow Park*, Christchurch Avenue, behind leisure centre, 0500
000020 (outdoor, free)

Horsham *Horsham Skatepark*, Hurst Road (outdoor, free) New, wooden
and floodlit

Ipswich *Bridge Park*, Bridge Street, next to Stoke Bridge,
www.ipswichskatepark.co.uk (outdoor, free) New concrete course
where you can pull off some East Angulars

Leigh-On-Sea *Leigh-On-Sea Park*, 2 Tree Lane, Essex, 07788 600896
(outdoor)

London *Cantaloes Park*, Camden Road, Camden (outdoor, free)

London *Meanwhile Gardens*, Elkstone Road, W10 (outdoor, free) The original park, near Royal Oak tube, was probably skated by your dad in the '70s – it was Europe's first concrete park. The newer one, close to PlayStation park, has three concrete bowls

London *PlayStation*, 60 Acklam Road, Ladbroke Grove, 0208 969 4669, www.pssp.co.uk (indoor-ish – under the motorway flyover) Tony Hawk just turned up unannounced here last year. That's really all you need to know about the brilliant PlayStation. Except that it's got a street course with every obstacle imaginable, a very scary vert ramp, a mini halfpipe set-up and beginners' sessions on Saturday mornings

London *Stockwell Bowl*, Stockwell Road, behind Brixton Academy, SW9 (outdoor, free) Been skating like a dream since the '70s

Maidenhead *The Matrix*, Kidwells Park, nr The Magnet Centre, 01628 796227 (outdoor, free)

Norwich *Extreme.Fun*, St Stephen's Street roundabout, Queens Road, 01603 611699 (indoor) Sprawling street course, plus an Internet café, so you can surf as well

Plymouth *Flatspot*, Clare Place, Coxside, 01752 222213 (indoor)

Portsmouth *Southsea Skatepark*, Southsea Common, Clarence Esplanade, 02392 825005 (outdoor, free)

Reading *Caversham Skatepark*, Hills Meadow, George Street (outdoor, free)

Redditch *Redditch Wheels*, Icknield Street (outdoor)

Romford *Rom Skatepark*, Upper Rainham Road, Hornchurch, Essex, 01708 474429 (outdoor) One of the best spots in the UK, with two bowls, a snake run, pool, halfpipe, ramps and moguls

Salisbury *Salisbury Skatepark*, Churchill Gardens (outdoor, free)

Saltash *Millennium Park*, Saltmill (outdoor, free)

St Albans *Pioneer*, Heathlands Drive, Harpenden Road, 01727 850741 (indoor) Brand new and one of the best undercover courses in the country

Taunton *Dreamfields*, The Exchange, Hamilton Road, 01823 325308, www.dreamfields.org.uk/ (indoor) No BMXs allowed. So go skate in peace

Totnes *Totnes Skate Park*, The Plain Playingfield, behind train station (outdoor, free)

Truro *Mount Hawke*, Gover Waterworks, 01209 890705 (indoor) Make like the Z-Boys and go when the Newquay waves aren't big enough for surfing

Wareham *Airborne Skatepark*, Industrial Estate Unit 11, 11 Sandsford Lane, Sandsford, 01929 550955, www.airbornuk.co.uk (indoor) New Skatelite park with halfpipes, quarterpipes, minis, grind box and rails. Plus a webcam so your mum can keep an eye on you from home

Waveney *East Coast Skatepark*, Colville House Youth Club, School Road, Oulton Broad, Lowestoft, Suffolk (outdoor) Street course and vert ramp

Weymouth *The Front*, Preston Beach Road, 01305 771301, www.sk8park.co.uk/ (outdoor)

Worthing *Worthing Skatepark*, Homefield Park (outdoor, free)

Yate *Peg Hill Skatepark*, 0117 914 7783, www.peghillskatepark.com (outdoor, free) Concrete bowl and street course 20 minutes outside Bristol

> ## "My favourite skatepark is St Albans. It's all new wood and they don't let bikes in so it doesn't get ruined. It's just really nice to skate."
> *Lucy Adams, 19, sponsored skater*

> *"The first time I went to PlayStation in London, I loved it. It's a whole different world."*
> *Jamie Holmes, 13, Reading*

SCOTLAND

Aberdeen *Beach Boulevard*, www.skateaberdeen.com (outdoor) Biggest halfpipe in Europe they say, plus huge street course

Clydebank *SK8TZ* at The Play Drome, 2 Abbotsford Road, 0141 951 4321,www.west-dunbarton.gov.uk/cats/CATS_Leisure_PD_SK8TZ. html (indoor, April to August)

Dundee *The Factory*, 44 Blinshall Street, Douglas Street, 01382 907117, www.factoryskatepark.com (indoor) Wooden street course, halfpipe and regular competitions. Get yourself on the BBC Online webcam

Livingston *Livingston Skatepark*, 16 Northwood Park, opposite Almondvale Shopping Centre, 01506 415308 (outdoor, free) Opened in the early '80s by Steve Caballero and the Bones Brigade, "Livi" is said to be the best skatepark in the UK

Perth *Perth Skate Park*, Lesser South Inch, Shore Road, www.pkc.gov.uk/skateparks/perth.htm (outdoor, free) Brand-new concrete bowls and quarterpipes

WALES

Caldicot *Caldicot Skatepark*, behind Sports & Leisure Centre, Monmouthshire, 01633 213219, www.caldicotsk8.fslife.co.uk (outdoor, free)

Cardiff *Cardiff Skatepark*, Rhymney Riverbridge Road, 02920 450359, www.cardiffskatepark.com (indoor)

Cwmbran *Cwmbran Skate Park*, near boating lake, Llanyrafon Way (outdoor)

Mold *Breaker's Yard*, Unit 4, Broncoed Business Park, Wrexham Road,

Flintshire, 01352 759990, www.thebreakersyardsk8park.co.uk (indoor)

Newport *Skate Extreme*, Herbert Road, 01633 265709 (indoor) With an 11.5-foot vert

Pontypridd *Sk8-X, Tynewydd Sidings*, Aberhondda Road, Porth, 01443 685577 (indoor)

Swansea *Swansea Skatepark*, Cwmdu Industrial Estate, Carmarthen Road, ann.price@swansea.gov.uk (indoor)

Tonyrefail *Dropzone*, Gilfach Road, mid-Glamorgan, 07789 763375 (indoor) Just opened an upstairs section after talks with local skaters

Wrexham *Daredevils Warehouse*, The Mold Road, Trading Estate, Gwersylld, 01978 312562 (indoor)

IRELAND

Bangor *Rampage Park*, Balloo Road, 02891 452166, www.rampagepark.com (indoor) With street course just for grommets

Dublin *Ramp City @ Kart City*, Old Airport Road, 0033 531 842 6322 (indoor)

Dublin *Ramp'n'Rail*, 96a Upper Drumcondra Road, 0035 301 837 7533, www.wayneslost.com (indoor)

Kilkenny *The Quarry*, Kiltorcan, Balyhale, 00353 566 8914, www.kartingireland.com (outdoor) Ireland's first outdoor skatepark has wooden ramps and concrete transitions. To come is a second street course, vert ramp and concrete clover bowl

NORTHERN IRELAND

Belfast *Rampage II*, Boucher Road, www.rampagepark.com (indoor) Northern Ireland gets a skatepark at last from the people behind the original Rampage in Bangor. Yay!

MEN AT WORK!

Parks are being built or rebuilt in **Castleford** (Allerton Bywater, www.bendcrete.com), **Burnley** (www.truckedup.co.uk/)

Halesworth, Suffolk (www.bandwskate.com), Hull (*Supa-Stadium*, http://sk8hull.blogspot.com), Leeds (*Hyde Park renovation*, www.lsb.org.uk), Leicester (*Doghouse*, www.casinoskates.com), Newquay (*Fearless Ramps*, www.skateparkpages.co.uk), Sunderland (*Gravity Projects*, 0191 514 2266), Workington (*Vulcan's Park*, email pennywize@talk21.com), Caerphilly (*Fearless Ramps*, 01865 408007), Strabane (*The Studio*, www.skateparkpages.co.uk), Edinburgh (*North Edinburgh Wheels*, www.newskatepark.moonfruit.com and Urban Revolution, www.urbanrevolution.homestead.com/home.html), Blantyre, Scotland (*Stonefield Park*, www.pkc.gov.uk/skateparks/blantyre.htm) and Stevenson, Scotland (01506 415308).

> ***"I started skating because I heard they were going to open up a park three blocks from my house ... That was 15 years ago and I haven't stopped since."***
> Bob Burnquist, pro skater

TARMAC VERY MUCH!

You don't have to part with your hard-swindled allowance to go skating – if you start looking at your local town sideways, you'll discover that the whole country's one giant skatepark. Places not intended for skating are always far more exciting than those that are. Curbs aren't for keeping the traffic off the pavement – they're for grinding on! Benches aren't for sitting on – they're for grinding on! Ledges aren't for . . . OK, OK, you've got the picture. Skateboarding was invented on a high street just like yours, not in some fancy state-of-the-art skatepark. So keep it real and take it back to the original streets. We're not talking actual streets, of course, as they've got dangerous metal boxes called cars tearing them up. No, you need to get off the beaten track. Check the UK skate mags like *Sidewalk* for locations. Look closely at all the photos to see whether or not you recognise any landmarks in the background that'll help you work out where the photo was taken. In your local area, look out for wax marks (usually black) on ledges and curbs, always telltale signs that a fellow skater's been there before you. Or check out that Internet site that has aerial photos of every street in the country for new spots without having to wear out your shoe leather. Here are just a few of the UK's best-kept skating secrets that won't cost you a penny. **Just stay on the right side of the law**.

ENGLAND

Birmingham Central Library, Chamberlain Square

Birmingham Centenary Square, Broad Street

Brighton Kingsway, from West Pier to Hove

Brighton Amex House, Edward Street

Bristol Lloyds Building, opp College Green

Doncaster Law Courts (next to Doncaster College)

Doncaster Train Station

Hull The Pond, Beresford Avenue (not in summer when it's full of water, though!)

Hull behind PC World, Clough Road Retail Park

Ipswich Suffolk College, Grimwade Street

Leeds West Yorkshire Playhouse, Playhouse Square, Quarry Hill

Leeds Millennium Square, Calverley Street

Leicester University, University Road

Leicester The Quay, Western Boulevard

London Euston Station, Euston Road

London Canary Wharf, Docklands

London Shell Centre, Belvedere Road

London Southbank, Queens Walk, under Waterloo Bridge

Manchester University, Oxford Road

Manchester Gasworks, Whitworth Street

Middlesbrough Civic Centre, Boulevard

Middlesbrough University of Teesside, Borough Road

Milton Keynes Central Train Station, Elder Gate

Milton Keynes The Beige

Newcastle Haymarket metro station, Haymarket

Newcastle University Of Newcastle Upon Tyne, Kings Walk

Newcastle-Under-Lyme Keele University, Keele Road

Norwich Gentleman's Walk, Theatre Street

Nottingham Trent University, Burton Street

Oxford Ice Rink, Oxpens Road

Oxford Institute of Virology, Mansfield Road

Plymouth Civic Centre, Armada Way

Portsmouth Pyramid Centre, Clarence Esplanade

Portsmouth Guildhall, Winston Churchill Avenue

Sheffield The Crucible Theatre, Arundel Gate

Sheffield Hallam University, Howard Street

Stoke Civic Offices, Glebe Street

> ***"I skate at Southbank for three hours a day and all weekend. I just go there and forget my worries."***
> *Tom Mills, 13, London*

SCOTLAND

Aberdeen University, St Machar Drive

Aberdeen Broad Street, just off Union Street, nr Castlegate

Dundee City Square, off High Street

Dundee Wellgate Centre, Victoria Road

Edinburgh Bristow Square, Potterow

Edinburgh Our Dynamic Earth, Holyrood Road

Glasgow George Square

Glasgow Gallery Of Modern Art, Queen Street

Livingston The Square, near skatepark

WALES

Cardiff Millennium Square, Maritime Road

Cardiff County Hall, Atlantic Wharf

Newport UWCN, Allt-yr-yn Avenue

Swansea Castle Square, Princess Way

Swansea University Of Wales, Singleton Park

IRELAND

Dublin Wood Quay, Winetavern Street

Dublin Central Bank, Dame Street

NORTHERN IRELAND

Belfast Waterfront, Oxford Street

Belfast Queen's University, University Street

"I've skated all kinds of terrain including streets and skateparks. I go all the way to Belfast and Lisnarrick and would go a lot further – it's the fun you get out of doing new stuff."

James, 13, Strabane

SKATING THE WEB

www.skateuk.net/places.asp The best slabs of tarmac in your town, reviewed by local skaters. It's actually for inline skaters, but hey, they nick our turf often enough.

www.knowhere.co.uk Type in your town and find a load of postings from local skaters arguing over the best places to skate.

Spots by Harry Bastard (£15, **www.thedopeshop.co.uk** or call 01273 240500) Harold leaves no paving stone unturned in his photo documentary of the UK's best street spots.

DIARY OF A PRO

Watch your heroes pulling off moves you can only dream about at the UK's top skateboarding events. Or enter yourself and give them a run for their money.

MAY

VAN'S KING OF STREET National Indoor Arena, Birmingham, 0121 767 2963, www.board-x.com. Midlands extravaganza boasts the biggest course in the country and skate-offs soundtracked by top DJs.

MID-JUNE

ALL LIVE SK8+ Springfield Park, London E6, www.stokenewingtonfestival.co.uk. Friendly, low-key, amateur skate contest with pro demos, workshops and skate gear.

EARLY SUMMER

LIVINGSTON'S PURE FUN SKATE PARTY Livingston Skatepark, 16 Northwood Park, 01506 415308. Weekend of events for all-comers. How meets used to be in the good ole days.

MID-JULY

BRISTOW SQUARE JAM Bristow Square, Edinburgh. For one cherished day a year this university square is transformed into a mini skate fest (check skate mags for details).

MID-JULY

NATIONAL ADVENTURE SPORTS SHOW Royal Bath and

West Showground, Shepton Mallet, Somerset, www.national-adventuresports.com. This massive extreme sports shindig is the biggest festival in Europe. There's skateboarding, snowboarding, wakeboarding, BMX, inline skating, mountain biking and even jet-skiing.

JULY

ESPN57 Aviemore 01343 550129, www.north57.com. THE event for riders in northeast Scotland with street and vert face-offs.

MID-SUMMER

SPRITE URBAN GAMES Clapham Common, London, www.board-x.com. Three-day urban culture festival with skateboarding, BMX, graffiti and hip hop.

AUGUST

CONCRETE CHALLENGE www.concretechallenge.com. Outdoor event that takes place in three UK skateparks every summer, with comps for all levels.

OCTOBER/NOVEMBER

RAMPWORX HALLOWE'EN JAM 1-3 Leckwith Road, Netherton, 0151 530 1500, www.rampworx2.co.uk. Frighteningly good all-nighter with hardcore tunes and hardcore skating.

NOVEMBER

BOARD-X Alexandra Palace, London www.board-x.com. Has now moved indoors to avoid the lame UK weather. Top European riders compete at street and vert.

SKATING THE WEB

Team Extreme tour the country giving skateboarding demos. Check out their schedule at **www.team-extreme.co.uk/schedule.html**.

HOLIDAY ON WHEELS

Are the 'rents arguing about where to go on holiday this summer? Why not suggest one of these fab destinations – just don't let on that all your enthusiasm is for the boarding spots.

Barcelona Tell the folks you're interested in Gaudi's architecture. And then go and investigate the marble architecture around Plaza de Cants. With your skateboard.

Marseilles Say you want to improve your French. Then improve your skating at the annual summer competition in the amazing concrete skatepark. Lyons, Montpellier and Paris are all great too.

Munster Feign an interest in German food like sauerkraut and sausages. It's a sacrifice, but it's worth it to go to the World Championships.

Rio de Janeiro, Brazil Develop an interest in carnival or football – your dad will be 100 per cent behind you on this one. Then leave him to it. The home of Bob Burnquist has more free, public concrete parks than any other country.

San Francisco, USA You've read about The Golden Gate Bridge at school and want to go see it. Nah, not really, you read that *Thrasher* magazine called San Francisco the "biggest skatepark in the world".

Sydney, Australia Just go on and on about the great

outdoors. Oz is the country that put vert skateboarders on a stamp in 1990. **Nuff said.**

Tampa, USA Holds a legendary skate comp every year. Unfortunately I can't think of any other reason to go there. Although it might be near Disneyworld.

Have a gander at the World Cup Skateboarding website at www.wcsk8.com/2002/schedule.lasso to find out where and when this year's events are taking place. Last year, the pros were picking up points in Melbourne, Vancouver, Copenhagen, Lausanne, Dortmund, Prague, Sao Paolo and around the USA. Helsinki, Malmo, Basel, Brussels and Seville are also skating meccas. But if your folks are really minted, get them to send you to skateboard camp in America. One of the best is run by Vans in Portland, Oregon between June and August (www.vansskatecamp.com/).

chapter eleven

Build your own ramp

Even if you're a fast learner, it's still going to take **a lot of knocks and bruises** before you're ready to tackle the local skatepark. Everyone there'll look as though they've been skating for ages and will have no patience with a beginner who keeps falling over and getting stuck under their new Ricta wheels. You might even do yourself a more serious injury.

Instead, get the hang of the basics in the privacy of your own driveway or back yard. A great way to master skatepark skills is to build your own ramp, slide bar or grind box. Then invite all your friends round and help each other learn. You can buy ramps and rails ready-made, but it's cheaper and far more rewarding to make them yourself. And if you rope the 'rents in, you could knock out a couple of launch ramps in a weekend, as 12-year-old Joe Turnbull found out . . .

Brian Perman, dad

"The trouble with skateboarding is that it's a slow progression from going down curbs to an enormous ramp in a skatepark. If you launch down one of those, you get a hell of a lot of acceleration and it's a bit scary. So building a ramp with Joe was quite useful in order to make the transition from horizontal skating to the vertical world of the skatepark.

"The other problem when you're nine or ten is that the bigger kids won't let you on the ramp anyway. So you need to make your own one to get good enough to go up there with them. We spent several Sundays knocking these ramps together. It was a good way of teaching Joe woodwork, which he's quite keen on. You can make a good ramp in about an hour and a half, but you need several so you can dot them around.

"Our fence had recently been repaired so we had a lot of four by two timber lying around, but it's not very expensive. Then you just use plywood or MDF for the surface. You need a certain thickness of ply because it bends, which can be fun, whereas MDF is solid. You've also got to have a saw that's sharp enough to cut MDF and to thin down the edge that's going to be flat on the ground.

"You can increase the height of the ramp by just nailing another bit of four by two on the bottom. Eight inches is the maximum – any more and it's too steep to get enough speed. Once your ramps get higher, you need to make sure that everything is well connected with three- or four-inch screws. And remember the down ramps need to be more solid than up ramps as you're going to land on them from a bit of height.

"When Joe was younger, the ramps worked very well. They lasted for three months or so. You can get all four wheels in the air and get the feel of landing at speed and of handling a ramp. It's a good way of practising the hair-raising stuff that comes later."

Joe Turnbull, son

"I decided to build my own ramp because I couldn't go to the skatepark every day. My dad and I built a big and a small ramp in about two and a half hours. It was a good feeling because I knew I'd built them myself and achieved something. Then I spray-painted pictures on them, kind of graffiti-style. It was when I'd just turned 10. At that age you're strong enough to do quite high ollies, to jump up and down and flip the board.

"I put the ramps on a hill and launched off the big one on to the small one. When you get more speed, you get higher and further. I learnt how to do ollies, 180s and kickflips off them. My friends came round and thought they were good too. We started off with a small gap and it just got bigger and bigger until we couldn't do it any more. Once someone lay down in the middle. He was kind of nervous, but we just ollied over him and it was fine.

"I don't really use the ramps any more because they're at my granny's and they're quite small for me now. But if I go and visit her, they're still good for mucking around on. I'd like to make some bigger ones sometime, when I get the right wood and stuff. I'd like to build a whole skatepark. It'd take a long time but I reckon I could do it.

"My favourite skatepark is PlayStation. I know quite a lot of people there and they teach me tricks, which is good because they're older and better than me. I like the halfpipe. When you skate down it you go really fast so you can do better tricks. I was a bit scared when I first stood on the top but after you've done it once, you're fine. It definitely helped that I'd practised on my own ramp."

MAKING PLANS

Fact One: all dads like DIY, and so do a surprising number of mums. **Fact Two:** all parents are big kids at heart. **Fact Three:** in reality, they'll do anything to get out of doing boring jobs round the house. So buy *Thrasher* magazine's *How To Build Skateboard Ramps – Halfpipes, Boxes, Bowls and More* (£7.50, www.amazon.co.uk) for your mum or dad's next birthday and persuade them to help you build a ramp in your back yard or (better still) garage away from the wind and rain.

Having problems persuading your parents? Don't fret. Tell them:

1. It'll help you with your schoolwork (maths, physics, woodwork).

2. It'll allow you to channel your artistic talents if you help with the design and layout.

3. It'll keep you fit.

4. It'll help you practise so you're less likely to get injured when you go for the big money moves down the skatepark.

5. It'll allow your parents to keep an eye on you when you go skating.

6. It'll help turn you into a responsible adult and teach you to take care of things. Like having a pet or something.

7. It'll help turn you into a skateboard megastar and they'll be able to retire and live off your millions.

The arguments are endless and, quite frankly, indisputable.

Start with maybe a grind box or slide bar, then move on to a ramp or quarterpipe, add a transition to wall, a funbox or pyramid and before you know it you've got half a skatepark in your drive. If you're really lucky, your dad'll develop a taste for it and offer to build you a vert ramp and bowl complex in the garden. Only problem is, after he's done it, he'll buy his own skateboard and spend the first three weeks embarrassing you as he tries to rediscover his youth.

 # SKATING THE WEB

HOME-MADE

www.heckler.com/ramps/index.html Free skateboard ramp plans from US magazine with down-to-earth advice on building funboxes, pyramids and halfpipes.

www.simplyskate.co.uk/ Easy plans for a launch ramp and quarterpipe.

www.skatoramps.com/ Buy plans for making your own skate ramps.

www.slapmagazine.com/new_site/woodshop/ Detailed plans for building mini-ramps, launchers, funboxes, quarterpipes, etc.

> *"I built a foot and a half wedge ramp that went from the patio on to the grass. There was work being done at my house so I nicked the builders' leftover bits of wood and things. If I got stuck, they hammered a nail in for me."*
>
> Lucy Adams, 19, sponsored skater

READY-MADE

www.argos.co.uk The Mike McGill slide bar costs £29.99.

www.kateskates.co.uk All kinds of ramps for sale.

www.routeone.co.uk Curved stunt ramp goes for £35 and a collapsible, 1.8m-long, adjustable-height grind rail is £39.95.

www.team-extreme.co.uk XTR Ramps make flat-packed kits for self-assembly. The grind box is £89, launch ramp £99 and flat bank £149.

"There's nowhere to skate in my area so I built a rail for myself and my younger brother Alex in the drive. I'm working on other stuff too now."
Sam Smith, 13, Fleet

"My parents built me a ramp in my back yard. My friends all come over and skate it."
Didier Ballan, 15, Billingshurst

chapter twelve
the Vans Groms

Are these the luckiest guys in the world? The Vans Groms are a group of skating prodigies hand-picked by team manager Christian Stevenson. They get free Vans gear, have just been on their first tour and are on the fast track to becoming pros.

Ross McGouran, 15, Harrow

"I was eight when I started, which is pretty young. I went to the skatepark with my BMX and then the local skate shop just gave me a board – I think I was a bit dangerous on a bike. It was fun and I kept at it. I made loads of friends who were a bit older than me so I learnt from them. My parents were OK about it – if I wasn't skateboarding, I'd probably be doing something else not so good.

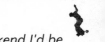

"I was down the skatepark loads. On a weekend I'd be there for about 10 hours and weekdays I'd skate for three or four. It took me about four months before I learnt to ollie but I learnt all the other basic tricks first – going up and down the ramps, turning – so when I did learn to ollie, I could do loads of other stuff from it.

"I used to enter as many competitions as I could, not just around my area. We'd go to places like Northampton as well. I entered my first one when I was nine and came third. Then I came sixth in the pro competition at the 2001 Urban Games when I was 13 and Christian asked me if I wanted to be with Vans. Since then, I came third in another pro contest, the 2002 NASS cup.

"I've broken my arm, chipped both my elbows and fractured my thumb. The worst was when I did my arm – it was all out of shape. I got up and was in real pain and they had to call an ambulance. It kind of put me off – you really have to build your confidence back up after something like that. I was out for seven weeks and was a bit rusty when I went back to the skatepark. **But the better you get, the more confident you are**.

"Skateboarding's fun. You can go wherever you want, you can do it whenever, it's free . . . If someone offered me the chance to be a pro, I wouldn't say no. I think normally it's your board company that turns you pro first, then your shoe company and so on. So you'd be sponsored by a number of companies and you'd be raking it in."

Harry Bray, 15, Newquay

"I was rollerblading for a year but I needed more of a challenge so I started skateboarding when I was 11. There's a lot more pain involved in the beginning, though.

In the summer I skate every single day, from 4 to 9.30pm. There's a little park over the road with a halfpipe and some ledges and we've built some boxes to go in there. If it's wet I'll go to Mount Hawke. My parents are really supportive – they always take me to skateparks or give me money to go places.

"I started skating mini-ramps first so learning to drop in and rock to fakies were my first tricks. I learnt them in just one night of hard core skating. Sometimes kids find it really hard to drop in but because I'd been blading first it gave me a head start, I wasn't scared to try stuff. The ollie and the heelflip took me about a week to get them, but only sketchy. It was probably about a month before I had them down.

"I hooked up with a little company down here called Homage Skateboards and they took me to Stoke Newington Festival in London. I came third and it went from there with Vans. I try to make every big competition I can now. Last summer I came fifth in the NASS one and won £75 – I even beat some of the adults so **I was really stoked** with that. When you go to these skate comps, all the people are real, real cool. There's good vibes going round – it's like one big family.

"I love the buzz of pulling off real good tricks. I love doing frontside flips and switch frontside flips. I've been trying to get these real big ones on the hip of a pyramid. I've got some good footage of that. The first photoshoot I did was in a magazine called Adrenaline, then there was The Face, and more recently I was in Sidewalk. I'm really stoked when I see photos of myself in magazines – I've worked hard for it.

"I'm trying not to get my hopes up but it would be

brilliant if I could make it pro. I'll keep entering competitions, but really it's all about having fun. If it doesn't happen, I'll try to get into the skateboarding industry – whether it's a clothing company or board company, anything just as long as it's to do with skating. Because it's just so amazing."

Trevor Beasley, 17, west London

"I could ollie the first day I bought my skateboard but then I'd been messing about on my friend's for a week. I was about 13. Now I work at PlayStation so I'm at the park nearly every day. Sometimes when it's closed, the people that work here all have a session together, which is great. Shell Centre is my favourite place, though. I'm in the skatepark all the time so it gets boring. Street skating is more motivating.

"I've known Ross for a while because he comes to PlayStation. When Christian was putting the Groms together at the Urban Games, Ross recommended me. We've just been on our first tour. It was fun, we were skating every day. When you've got people of all different standards, it pushes you to do even harder tricks.

"If I can't go skating, I'll sit at home and play Pro Skater 4. It's the best one yet. There's more game play, better tricks, and it's harder. If you're learning to skate, it can even give you tips when you're doing ollies and stuff, to land straight and keep your balance. And if you want to learn a new trick, you can just go on the game, see how it's done and then try it yourself on your board.

"I think a good skateboarder is someone who lands their tricks consistently and isn't a show-off – we get a few of them down at PlayStation.

My favourite skater is Jamie Thomas. His style, the way he skates, he's a proper chilled-out skater. I've actually met him and he's really friendly. I don't want to be a pro, though. I think amateurs make more money – in some comps you can win £10,000. So if someone asked me to be a pro, I'd say no."

"I'd like to be a professional, but it'll take me a long time."
Jake Ponting, 10, Wiltshire

FUNBOX FUNBOX FUNBOX FUNBOX
DID YOU KNOW?

Impress your mates with your intimate, in-depth knowledge of skateboarding. Even if you don't even know how to kickturn yet.

1. Early slalom and downhill contests were held in London Underground tunnels and Brands Hatch motor racing track.

2. Pro skater Steve Alba's cousin is Jessica Alba from *Dark Angel* and Steve Berra is married to Hollywood filmstar Justine Lewis.

3. Rodney Mullen was only ever beaten once in freestyle competitions – in 1983 by Sweden's Per Welinder.

4. Japanese police use portable rubber mats to stop skaters using street spots.

5. Brazilian Bob Burnquist has a Skatelite course in his garden.

FLYNN

"I haven't had to have a proper job for over seven years. It's been amazing. I feel stoked to have been able to have the skater's lifestyle."

Flynn Trotman, pro skater

6. Eating oily fish like mackerel helps strengthen your knees for skating.

7. Oxford Council dumped 30 tonnes of sand on to a skatepark last year after residents complained it was too noisy. It had cost them £32,000 to build and was open for just six weeks.

8. *Jackass'* Johnny Knoxville used to work for *Big Brothers* magazine.

9. Vert king Andy Macdonald gives away his board after competitions to the first kid who can show him a library card.

10. Shawn Hacking was knocked off his skateboard by a flying goose. The 13-year-old Canadian's friend Brent Bruchanski said: "It was so funny. It flew out of nowhere and then . . . bam!"

chapter thirteen

So you want to get paid to Skate?

Aaah, join the queue. It's every skater's dream –
travelling the world entering competitions, all your boards
and clothing free, being able to skate every day and
not having to worry about getting up before 2pm to go
and photocopy files and make tea or whatever it is other
people do.

There really is no particular strategy for getting
sponsored, but there are various simple ways to improve
your chances. Firstly, just enjoy your skating and don't get
too obsessed with your dream. Skate every hour God
sends. And then borrow some from the devil. Get high
placings in competitions, but if the phone's still not ringing
don't start bawling out your little brother to get off the
Internet. Especially if you've got broadband. It takes time.

Just enter more competitions – they're a great way to monitor how good you are compared to your peers.

Secondly, get some photos of yourself in a magazine or make a video. With any luck, one of your pals will be a budding photographer or film-maker. Find a spot that you've never seen anyone skate before and make it your own. Films should be short and sweet. Skate companies get so many home-made videos that they're not going to sit through 15 minutes to get to your grand finale. If you're conquering new terrain and pulling off original tricks with style, you'll raise some eyebrows.

Include some details about yourself – skate companies are looking for outgoing personalities who will represent their brand enthusiastically and responsibly. Most important of all, make sure your video reaches the right person. Check websites, or phone to find out the correct name and address. There's no point going to all that effort and then having your video end up in the bin because it went to the accounts department.

Getting sponsored is the first step to becoming a pro. The company will give you a certain amount of gear per year, whether it's boards, shoes, backpacks or even bagels (see Chapter 14). Usually, you'll get more free stuff than you can use so you can make a bit of wonga selling it on to your friends. Apart from the bagels, of course. Once you've got a deal with one company, it should be easier to get others on, er, board.

For the hallowed few who make it and turn pro, you'll get a monthly pay packet on top of all the freebies. But let's not run before you can spacewalk. The main thing is just to go out there and skate and have fun with your pals. If you're good enough, sponsors will come to you.

THE PROS
Meet the guys who are living the dream

Manuel Palacios, 30, Madrid

"You get paid for doing what you like so it's cool. It's not hard – a couple of demos, a couple of shows, try to get your picture printed in magazines . . . I don't really like to see photos of myself, though. You always think you could have done the trick a little better.

"I was 26 when I became pro. This guy started a new skateboard company and just asked if I wanted to ride for them. I'd been doing competitions for a long time – I won the Spanish championships in street and vert in '93 and '94 and did well in Europe, but now I can take it easier, relax . . . I don't really like competing. I had to quit skating for eight months because I broke a ligament in my knee. But I kept on doing promotions and stuff and all my sponsors supported me, especially Quiksilver – they really took care of me.

"We mainly move in Europe but every year there's some strange location to go to – it's nice. The weirdest was Morocco – there's not even a good surface, but it was fun. A great atmosphere and nice people. We went to Casablanca and then toured the country, just skating down the street. The locals were amazed. It's like when you're younger and someone comes to your park from outside, it's always nice to see what they can do.

"If you want to become a pro, style, technique and the difficulty of the tricks you perform are all important. The best skateboarders have all that to varying degrees. Whether they mainly do rails, stairs, whatever, they can really flow with a skateboard. For me, **style is the most crucial thing**. One trick can be done differently by 30 people. That's skateboarding.

"I also snowboard every winter. I'm sponsored with the same kind of deal as skating. But I enjoy skateboarding more – there aren't so many conditions like money, car, weather, snow, housing, ticket . . . I want to keep skating as long as I can. I will have to change rhythm soon and start focusing on different things, but maybe I'll still have a little mini-ramp when I'm 60 and just cruise by."

Tomi Toiminen, 31, Helsinki

"I took up skating around 1985 when I was 16 – kind of a late start. I had a summer job in a warehouse and one guy brought this little skateboard back from America and used to cruise round on it picking up stuff from the shelves. I started playing around with that and then my friends all bought boards. We built a vert ramp because there was nothing in Helsinki. We didn't have a clue how to do it and it was uneven but it worked OK. There were a few older guys on the other side of town who made a ramp too, out in the forest.

"At first my dad was really against it, but he couldn't say anything because I saved up to buy my own board. I did well in a few contests and he realised that maybe it was a good thing. I won the Finnish championship and in 1988 went to the European Championships – it was my first street contest abroad and I came fifth. The next year I came sixth in Copenhagen against all these pros and hooked up with Powell-Peralta. The year after that I started doing demos with Tony Hawk.

"Tony was one of my heroes. The Bones Brigade and Powell movies always had the best skaters, so it was a dream come true but I was a little nervous. Back then when you did a demo there were loads of people watching and afterwards we'd have an autograph session. **I'd be sitting next to Tony Hawk** writing my name thinking, 'I bet you don't know who I am.' It was weird. But he's super cool, a really nice guy.

"About four years ago I signed up with Quiksilver. I ride for them and Vans and Lib Tech skates and snowboards – I've been a professional snowboarder for 10 years. I actually quit skateboarding while I was concentrating on snowboarding and then got the bug again four or five years ago. Now I can't have one without the other.

"The best way to get sponsored is to let your riding speak for itself. Go to contests as they're a good way to meet people and get known. But at the end of the day, competitions are not so important. Usually if you're a good skater and you go round a bunch of different places, word will spread. So skate everything and keep the fire going. There's never an end to what you can do."

> **"You can't go on stage and sing with Michael Jackson, yet you can skate the same handrail or the same skatepark as Koston, Muska or Kirchart with the possibility of them being there."**
> *Steve Berra, pro skater*

Genaro Vergoglini, 29, New Jersey

"A lot of kids today expect to be able to do everything they see in the magazines, which is extremely difficult and takes a lot of practice. It took me about eight months to get my board off the ground. So just be patient and have fun with your friends. I'd go out skating all day until I heard my mum whistling down the block for dinner. You forget about everything. You don't think about school or girls or this and that, you just focus on having fun and trying to do the latest move. When you make a kickflip over the box and all your mates are yelling, it's a really cool high that you can't get any other way.

"I put together a video and sent it to Trust, a new board company that was starting up, and they took me on as an amateur. It was cool to be part of something that wasn't already established. I was 18 or 19 when I first started getting free stuff. You get a knock on the door and it's really exciting. Within a year I was a pro. The best thing was the travelling. I went to Sweden and the Czech Republic – it was so cool to see all these kids skating. **There was this Czech kid riding a board with my name on it and it really freaked me out**.

"My favourite skater is Mike Carroll. He has the cleanest style and finesse and his feet are always perfect when he lands, which I love. I like to see kids who I've never seen before just come to the local park and cruise around with a really nice style doing unique tricks. They don't have to do the craziest tricks or the biggest jumps. I'll see someone just pushing and riding and be like, 'That guy is awesome, just the way he carves.'

"These days I play drums in a band called The Pleased. Skateboarding helped a lot with my co-ordination and drumming came pretty naturally. But I still ride for Adrenaline Skateboards out of Grass Valley, California. There's a great new local park and I'll go three times a week. It's so much fun – I'm almost 30 but I still feel like a little kid, but I guess that's skateboarding for you. The photo on the front of this book was actually taken at Grass Valley. I'm about to do one of my favourite tricks – a backside ollie."

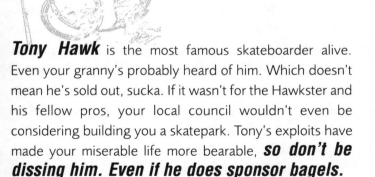

chapter fourteen
the world's greatest

Tony Hawk is the most famous skateboarder alive. Even your granny's probably heard of him. Which doesn't mean he's sold out, sucka. If it wasn't for the Hawkster and his fellow pros, your local council wouldn't even be considering building you a skatepark. Tony's exploits have made your miserable life more bearable, ***so don't be dissing him. Even if he does sponsor bagels.***

Tony Hawk has achieved more in skateboarding than anyone else – bar none. He's retired from the competition circuit now, but in his day he took part in over 100 contests, winning 73 and coming second in 19 (that's way better than anyone else), ruled almost every vert competition since 1982 and collected 10 X Games gold medals to hang over his mantelpiece. Or pin on his jacket or something. He landed the world's first ever 900 (that's two-and-a-half turns mid-air off a vert ramp) and is said to have invented more tricks than any other skater, including 540s, kickflip 540s, varial 540s, 720s, the stalefish grab and the Madonna grab. And with Andy Macdonald as his partner, he won the X Games vert doubles for the fifth year in a row in Philadelphia in 2001.

Tony started skateboarding when he was nine after his older brother Steve gave him a blue fibreglass banana board. Two years later, he gave up baseball to concentrate on skating. Despite looking like a flimsy beanpole, he became the youngest pro at 14 and was winning competitions two years later. He became an original member of the Bones Brigade and the money he earned from prizes, videos and sponsorship enabled him to buy a house aged 17. A year later, he'd toured the world twice and had his own signature skateboard.

These days the 34-year-old lives in California in a specially designed house with ramps outside and interior floors that you can skate on. He has three sons – the oldest, Riley, started skateboarding before he could walk. Which isn't that surprising, considering he was probably born with a skateboard genetically attached to his feet. Despite having to change nappies, Tony still finds time to skate two hours a day and run a global skateboarding empire.

His latest venture is the **Boom Boom Huck Jam**, a touring extreme sports extravaganza featuring vert skating, BMX and Motocross choreographed together while bands like Offspring and DEVO play live. "It's constant action, constant excitement," says Tony. "Hopefully people will come to see something unique and exciting and then leave having seen stuff way beyond what they expected." And that's Tony Hawk for you.

MAD TONY TRIVIA

1. He comes from good blood – his explorer ancestor Henry Hudson Hawk discovered Canada's Hudson Bay. And dad Frank ran the National Skateboard Association in America in the '80s, organising some of the first pro and am contests. And no, that's not why Tony won. He was better than everyone else.

2. Tony joined an elite group of US celebs, including former president Bill Clinton, when he did an advert for milk wearing the famous white milk moustache. He's also starred in an ad for Apple computers.

3. His computer game, Pro Skater, makes him over $6m in royalties per year.

4. Tony aired over a police car in *Police Academy 3*.

5. The Tony Hawk Foundation provides cash to build public skateparks in the US.

6. He guest-starred in the 300th episode of *The Simpsons* (it's called "Barting Over"), shown in America in February 2003. Presumably as Toony Hawk?

7. Tony is sponsored by Bagel Bites – a chain of bread shops in America.

8. Our hero plays himself in recent Hollywood comedy, *The New Guy*. See Chapter 18 for more of Tony's attempts to shred Tinseltown.

9. Tony spent $1m of his own money building the state-of-the-art ramps and stage sets used in Boom Boom Huck Jam.

10. You can buy a radio-controlled Tony Hawk skateboard toy. Use the remote to vary Tony's body position as well as the board to make him do tricks – or if you've got a mean streak, make him wipe out time after time.

"My first impression of Tony was that he was small and weak. He was so noodle-like, everything he did seemed to require heroic effort. No one was putting money on him for future champion."

Stacy Peralta, pro skater

"Every time people who don't know anything about skating find out I'm a skater, they say, 'Do you know the guy that did the 900?' Tony helped take it to the next level, to where it won't die again."

Chad Muska, pro skater

FUNBOX FUNBOX FUNBOX FUNBOX
RECORD-BREAKERS

1. Longest and highest air At the Op King of Skate contest on 17 April 2002, Danny Way flew 65 feet in the air. The next day he jumped 18 feet 3 inches (5.56m) off a quarterpipe to set another world record. Five years earlier, the fearless legend jumped out of a helicopter on to a special vert ramp in Las Vegas. He's not super-human though – the first time he tried it he dislocated his shoulder and "smacked my face on the bottom of the ramp, harder than I ever have in my life". But not being one to give up, he just dusted himself off, got back in the helicopter and pulled it off on his second attempt.

2. Most mid-air rotations Tony Hawk's 900 at the X Games in San Francisco on 27 June, 1999. He finally landed the stunt on his 12th attempt.

3. Fastest Gary Hardwick from California reached 62.55mph (over 100kph) in a race at Fountain Hills, Arizona on 26 September 1998. When he wasn't breaking records, he relaxed by jumping 50-foot gaps at 50mph on a board with skyhooks. Hmm, that's probably a record too.

4. Fastest jet-propelled Billy Copeland reached 70mph (112.65kph) on 15 May 1998 on a street luge in Bakersfield, USA. He had no brakes so he strapped a piece of tyre to his trainers to slow himself down.

5. Furthest distance travelled on a skateboard is 271.3 miles by the bizarrely named Eleftherior Argiropoulus in Greece. It took him one and a half days. Which is about the same amount of time it takes to introduce himself.

6. Furthest distance jumped between two skateboards Tony Alva launched himself 19 feet (5.8m) over 17 barrels.

7. Highest and longest ollie from flat ground The highest is 44.48 inches (113cm) by the UK's very own Danny Wainwright on 6 February 2000 at Long Beach, California. Danny also holds the record for the longest ollie, set at Glissexpo in Paris 2000, when he jumped over 15 feet.

8. Largest skatepark is The Vans Skatepark in Prince William, Virginia. It covers 61,640 square feet (5,726.5 sq m) and opened in April 2000.

9. Most expensive deck ever bought was an Original Powell Peralta Mint Tony Hawk from 1983. Collector Vince Spiceland sold it for US$6,000 on ebay.

10. Youngest ever sponsored skateboarder is five-year-old Mitchie Brusco from Seattle, who is on the books of six skateboard companies. When asked if he wanted to become pro one day, he said, "Maybe when I'm 10."

chapter fifteen
sistas are doing it for themselves

Cruise around any skatepark these days and you'll see more and **more girls**. And not just hanging around the coffee machine. Last year, all-girl contests were introduced to the UK at King Of Street (the cleverly named Queen Of Street), and the second Girls Skate Out, where the whole of Birmingham's Epic skatepark was taken over by female riders, took place in February. The first all-girl skate vid, *AKA: Girl Skater* (see Chapter 18), has also just hit the shelves, featuring Jamie Reyes, Vanessa Torres (World Champion 2001), Amy Caron (World Runner-Up 2001) and Monica Shaw (Australian champion). Clearly girls aren't so keen on netball any more.

But female skaters have been around since lipstick was invented. One of the original Z-Boys was really a girl. Peggy Oki was asked to join after she was spotted thrashing a board her brother had made in woodwork class. "I have been a tomboy all my life so I didn't get intimidated," says Peggy. "I felt like one of the guys. They were doing all these things and so was I. As far as falling, getting scraped up or bruised – that never bothered me. So they probably saw that I wasn't some little girl. That brought me respect."

The first All Girl Skate Jam – no smelly testosterone allowed – was held in America in 1997 and it's now an annual event which tours the globe. Laura Powell and Vanessa Gorman organised a UK version in Sheffield last year. One of the stars of the Brit scene is Lucy Adams, who won the King Of Street competition. Her sister, Rosie, was the youngest to enter at just 11 and her dad runs a skateboard shop in Horsham. This particular Adams family must have some extremely baggy genes.

Lucy Adams, 19, Horsham

"When I was 13 I used to go to a swimming club in Crawley and they were building a skatepark at the back of the leisure centre. Before it was officially open, I climbed through the fence with my rollerboots. These guys told me that if I got a skateboard then they'd let me on the ramps. I don't expect they thought I would. But every Friday before swimming I'd go to the skatepark and practise for an hour or so. When I was old enough, I started going every weekend. I was the only girl but it didn't bother me. There were a lot of beginners and we all learnt together. No one gave me any hassle.

"At the beginning, I just skated this one four-foot mini-ramp. A year later I found out I hadn't learnt quite a lot of the basics, like I didn't know how to ollie. Then it got harder because I'd missed out on so much. But I learnt it and whenever somebody did a new trick, I'd want to learn that too.

We all just pushed ourselves. I don't know if boys care that I'm a girl – we're all just skateboarders, part of the same gang.

"It was actually the same guy who'd told me to get a skateboard instead of rollerskates who ended up sponsoring me. He worked at 360 Clothing and after I did well in a few of the Crawley competitions I got free jeans and T-shirts from them. Then he put me in touch with Gallaz shoes. I hooked up with Nikita Clothing and then after winning King Of Street in 2002, I got sponsored by Eastpak and Reaction.

"After that I went to the Etnies European Open in Paris and came fourth. The girl who won, Ianire Eloriagga, is amazing, a real park skater. It made me want to learn what she did. I tried it and I could do it. I realised that even though she beat me, she's not out of my reach. She came fourth in the World Cup in 2002 so I've got a chance of doing well there too. I'd like to see some of the US pros skate because if a girl is doing something, I've always got to give it a go – it's like if she can do it, so can I.

"I hope more girls get into skateboarding. They shouldn't worry about what boys think. Just go to the skatepark and watch other people. It's best to have a group of friends to do it with and push each other to learn new tricks. Style is important, you need good balance and you have to have a lot of guts to jump down big ramps. Anyone can pick it up, but it takes a better person to go all the way with it.

"People say that if more girls get good at skating, then it'll look better – more elegant. Girls have finesse because we practise a trick until we perfect it. Boys don't worry about that. They just throw themselves down stairs, or do millions of tricks, no matter how bad they look."

Ianire Eloriagga, 20, Bilbao

"I started because I saw my older brother Xabier skateboarding and he's really good. I was about 14. In the Basque country, there aren't many girls boarding, but there are more than in other parts of Europe. My favourite place to skate is Bilbao. The first time I came to England when I won Board X last year, it just rained the whole time.

"If I wasn't skateboarding, I'd be playing football. I gave it up when I started skateboarding seriously. I really enjoy skating – it's a sport too and it's really healthy. I feel lucky when I learn a new trick and when I see other people skate, inspiration comes to me. I don't know whether I'm popular with the boys. Sometimes they stare, but they don't get annoyed if I'm better than them. If girls want to do it, they should give it a go. If you don't do something you enjoy, life is boring."

Amy Ram, 14, Fulham, London

"Most girls haven't touched a skateboard in their lives. I think it's because it's dangerous. I haven't broken anything, but I get loads of cuts and bruises on my arms. It doesn't put me off, though. I know maybe four girls who skate. In a way it's good because I'm kind of original. You get a lot of attention and the boys all want to talk to you. I go to an all-girls school and I like to get away from them once in a while!

"I started almost two years ago. I used to blade, but it was too easy so I decided to take up a challenge. PlayStation park is my favourite place – I can skate the vert ramp now. I entered a competition last June and won the mini-ramp section and came second in another one in August, but I also won best trick. I wouldn't mind being a professional – I've seen how Elissa Steamer is so rich. I've written to some sponsors, but they haven't replied yet. My friends are sponsored by Gallaz but I'm better than them."

"Girls say that it's easier to go and skate in parks where there are other girls. There's quite a lot of networking and everyone knows each other. But I'd rather be seen as just another skateboarder."
Jenna Selby, 23, St Albans

"I like to skate, it's fun. I skateboarded in high school and I like to do it in my free time. It's not like I'm a pro. I fall a lot, but I mean, everyone falls, you know."
Avril Lavigne

"My favourite trick is to indy over the jump box, but anyone starting out should learn to ollie even if they want to ride ramps."
Rosie Adams, 12, Horsham

"When a girl does decent tricks, it gets noticed. Whether you stand out because you're a girl, have sparkly rimless glasses, an Afro or a leather jacket – you still stand out. In that way it has helped me."
Jessie Van Roechoudt, pro skater

SKATING THE WEB

www.girlsskateout.co.uk News, competitions, links, message board and database of contact details of other girl skaters in the UK

www.girlsskatebetter.com News and trick tips from our American sistas

www.frontsidebetty.com Girl action from the US

www.pushskatemag.com Check out this new glossy mag for girls – no, not *ELLEgirl*, it's a skate mag called *Push*

chapter sixteen
a design for life

Unfortunately very few of us end up making it as a skater and, let's face it, if we were all pros, life would be boring. You'd probably end up wanting to be a bus conductor instead. But there are other ways to hang with some of the coolest dudes on the planet and that's by getting a career in the industry. You already know enough about the skating scene – all you need now is a splash of artistic talent and a rucksack full of determination. We're not talking about working in a skate shop here – any two-bit punk with an attitude problem can do that. We're talking *photography, design and film-making*.

If you've been inspired enough to take up skateboarding in the first place, you've already got a headstart. According to Z-Boy-turned-Tinseltown film mogul Stacy Peralta, skaters see the world differently to others. When we look at a new shopping centre being built, we see beauty and potential in the smooth concrete surfaces, while everyone else just sees a pile of bricks and mortar and yet another Starbucks. Plus the sport itself is endlessly creative. **There are no rules** so you really need to use your imagination to interpret your surroundings.

By videoing his Z-Boy pals with a handheld camera and setting his films to a kicking soundtrack, Stacy set the standard for extreme sports videos and created a style of filming that has even crossed over into Hollywood action blockbusters. Spike Jonze, director of *Being John Malkovich* and pop videos like Fatboy Slim's *Praise You*, also started out with skate footage and 1991's *Video Days* is still a must-see (see Chapter 18). With today's modern digital technology, it's easier and cheaper than ever to make your own film. And with demand for skateboarding footage higher than a Danny Way vert stunt, there's never been a better time to warm the director's chair.

The same goes for design and graphics. Over the years, skateboards have had all kinds of bizarre incarnations from fishtails to hammerheads but these days, most companies have put the gimmicks back in the funbox and stopped squabbling over the basic shape. Which pretty much means that the only way to tell your skateboard from your mates' is the graphics on the darkside. With more skate companies around than ever, the quality and originality of logos and designs has become crucial if they want to sell their boards and art departments are always on the lookout for new Mac wizards.

So if you're a budding Craig Stecyk, Mark Gonzales or Ed Templeton (they all designed their own decks), start by customising your own board. Buy a blank wooden deck, play around with art programs on the computer and come up with your own design. Then paint or spray it on to your board. Get inspiration from design bookshops like Magma, graffiti art or the Internet and develop your own style. One thing's for sure, you'll certainly stand out from all those Teeny Hawk clones.

Don't be too precious about your design though, 'cos it'll get thrashed after half a dozen sketchy boardslides. Look on the bright side – it'll give you the chance to develop your ideas further. **It's a work in progress, dahling!** Before long, your mates will be asking you to do graphics for them and you'll be the entrepreneur on the block. Except way, way cooler than Virgin's Richard Branson. Experiment with different styles for your pals' boards. Then, if you haven't already been noticed, get all your designs together in a portfolio (it looks all professional-like) and send them to your favourite skate companies. Then sit back and wait for your new career to take off. And laugh at all your mates working the tills down Tesco.

FUNBOX FUNBOX FUNBOX FUNBOX
ART ATTACK

If you're the kind of drongo who keeps forgetting to take the lens cap off, why not win the country's biggest art prize instead? That's exactly what 28-year-old skater and Glasgow skatepark designer Toby Paterson did last year, when his 69-foot mural "We Fall Into Patterns Quickly" scooped the £24,000 Beck's Futures Award, the alternative to the Turner Prize. A much richer Toby said afterwards that his painting had been inspired by his street-shredding adventures. As opposed to the rest of us, whose only inspiration after a hard day's skating is to go and get a Big Mac.

SNAP HAPPY

Dominic Marley is a skater. He also takes photos. And he's just started to get his work published by *Sidewalk* magazine. He's not related to Bob, though.

"I was into photography before I took up skateboarding so taking skate photos just seemed natural. In 2000 I took a photo of my friend Jacob, who was sponsored by Carhartt. They asked me to do some more and sorted out film, expenses and processing bills and that summer, I just took skate photos all the time. Carharrt displayed my prints in the London shop for a while, which was cool.

"Getting a good skate photo is about perseverance – there's a lot of waiting about. There's two ways to do it. You can either just snap away or you can collaborate with the skater, get them to work around your lights. I don't really like shooting in skateparks – they're boring. I prefer to use something different in the city, maybe just a bench. So you've got people sitting on it one day and people skating on it the next.

"Some of the newer SLR cameras have motor drives on them, which are good for sequences, something you've got to do these days if you're taking skate photos. Usually they're anything from five to ten frames a second and basically you just hold the button down and go through a lot of film. It costs a lot of money so you've got to have some idea that the skater's going to do the trick.

"You get opportunities to photograph the big names – they're always floating about – but I prefer shooting my friends. You can always ask them to go and re-do something! Then send your photos in to a magazine and explain you're just starting out. Chances are they'll get back to you on a positive note. I found *Sidewalk* really helpful. They told me what they liked and what they didn't and told me how to get the most out of what I was shooting.

"I've had a few photos in *Sidewalk* already and I'm trying to do a lot more for them. It's difficult in this country because of the weather, especially over the winter. Some people go off and take snowboarding photos, but you need different techniques for that because of the light reflecting off the snow. I'd rather go somewhere hot and take skate photos.

"There is a move towards digital photography at the moment – I suppose it's a lot quicker as you don't have to set up lights – but I'm happy as I am. The quality isn't even close to film at the moment. In a few years I'll know whether I can earn a living out of it. I hope so – it's what I love."

 ## SKATING THE WEB

www.graphotism.com/cgi-local/shop/range.cgi?range=paints Buy your spray cans here

www.jazi.ch Top graffiti art site from Switzerland

www.magmabooks.com Online version of design bookshop. Great for inspiration

www.skateboardgraphics.com Skateboard graphics and designs throughout the ages

chapter seventeen
common threads

Over the past 20 years, **skatewear** has been adopted by no end of hangers-on who've never even been near a halfpipe, let alone owned a board. These days you'll see every Tom, Dick or Kev in a pair of Vans, baggy jeans and Slipknot hoodie. What they don't understand is that skating has never been about what brands you wear or who you listen to. Like skating, it's all about freedom of expression and personal taste. Skate "fashion" was born out of the practical needs of anyone down the skatepark. If we didn't wear skate clothes, we'd get cuts and bruises. Or cold. Or arrested for public indecency.

The crossover began in the '80s with brands like Vision Street Wear, Airwalk and Stüssy while skull, snake and dragon designs inspired by board graphics also became popular. The early '90s saw the return of old-skool Adidas, Puma and Converse trainers, while baggy clothes worn by skaters for freedom of movement made the high street a laughing stock. Blind jeans, the first to be unhemmed so you could customise the length, were also adopted, er, blindly. By the late '90s, the popularity of the Beastie Boys had led to DC Shoes becoming a household name, while Etnies was everywhere. These days, even Nike has a skate team, although it's taken a while for the brand to break into the skate scene.

One company that's always been close to the heart and sole of skating, however, is Vans. When skaters get up in the morning, the first thing they put on is their trainers (that's if they've actually taken them off). But it wasn't always like this. The earliest skaters didn't even wear shoes – hey, you didn't when you were surfing – but they quickly saw sense when they found out that concrete was a whole lot harder than water. Especially when Vans came along in 1966 with some new trainers that were strong, flexible and grip-tastic. They were perfect for skateboarding.

Vans hooked up with the Z-Boys and Stacy Peralta became the first skater to get paid to wear a brand of trainers. Once a month, he'd run to the little corner store in Santa Monica to pick up a new pair. And so skate sponsorship was born. All these years later, you still can't go far wrong with Vans. They've been there and done that before you were even born. But we're not going to tell you how to dress – we'll leave that to your mum.

SHOE FLY

1. Your trainers will take a lot of punishment around the little toe area when you ollie so make sure this part is well protected. Hot glueing, triple stitching and lace protectors could all make them last longer. But don't get soles that are too thick, otherwise you won't feel the board.

2. Shoegoo is liquid rubber that comes in a tube and is sold in skate shops. It'll plug any gaping holes in your Scoobys and works surprisingly well. Alternatively, try the bizarrely named Vloeibare Zool, which should be available from most hardware stores. But please can we be there when you ask for it?

3. Having problems doing tricks? Astound your friends with Magnatron's shoes and board (www.magnatronskate.com). It'll feel like you've got magnets in your shoes – oh, you have.

THE SKATER'S UNIFORM

Trainers Always on last legs as well as yours

Jeans or combats Preferably not the ones you wear on Saturday nights

Canvas belt To keep low-slung trews from getting in the way of tricks

Key or wallet chain So you don't lose 'em when you're ollieing over that drainage ditch

Shockproof watch To get you home in time for tea

Skateboard logo T-shirt Freebie from mate who's sponsored

Baggie hoodie To protect your arms from grazes. Why? Because you're worth it

Beanie or helmet Because the UK weather's bound to take a turn for the worse

Wrap radio Turn on, tune in and cop out. Just don't get it stuck on Magic FM (check www.soundspecs.com/)

Rucksack Briefcases just aren't practical when you're doing grabs

---

FUNBOX FUNBOX FUNBOX FUNBOX
WHAT YOU'LL FIND IN A SKATEBOARDER'S RUCKSACK

1. First Aid kit, including finger splints, plasters and antiseptic cream

2. Copy of *Sidewalk* magazine

3. Broken-off piece of ramp once skated by Tony Hawk

4. Map with all the local skate spots circled

5. Mobile phone that takes photos – to catch your mates' sickest stunts

6. Four-pack of Red Bull, so you don't have to take a break

7. CD of skate tunes downloaded from the Internet

8. Library card, in case you bump into Andy Macdonald (see Chapter 12)

9. Candle for impromptu curb waxing

10. Reward card from local KFC

"In the summer one pair of skate shoes would only last me about two weeks."
Lucy Adams, 19, sponsored skater

chapter eighteen
videos, music, magazines, games...

So it's bucketing with rain again. Stop moaning and get used to it – you live in England (let's not even get started on Scotland, Wales and Ireland). Don't despair. Apart from spending your life savings on a flight to the south of France, there are still many skate-related things you can do while you wait for the sun to get his hat back on again.

SIGHTS

Skate videos have become mighty big business over the past ten years and there's a bewildering array of titles out there. To help you sort the ones that are sick from the ones that suck, have a look at the following list, which has some of the best skate videos ever made. Many of the old classics are now being re-released on DVD so you might get lucky and find them in your local skate shop.

Otherwise, check the Internet or ask around the park and swap with fellow skaters to save yourself some serious dollar. Only when you've exhausted all your mates' collections is it worth shelling out on your own.

If you're not sure what to look for, keep a lookout for videos featuring footage of the world's best skaters. Tom Penny was an expert at street skating, Chad Muska has tamed most of the world's rails, Tony Hawk and Bob Burnquist rule vert, while Mark Gonzales, Geoff Rowley, Andrew Reynolds and Jamie Thomas are all just insane. Then make yourself a cup of tea, break out a packet of Hobnobs, switch on the electric fire and settle back into the armchair. Have the remote handy so you can use the slow-mo to pick up top trick tips from the pros. Soon you'll have forgotten all about the weather.

SKATING VIDEOS

411 Video Magazine (www.411vm.com) Already past its 50th issue, *411* prescribes a never-ending dosage of top footage of contemporary pro skaters. Number Six featured our cover star, Genaro Vergoglini

Mix Tape (Zoo York, set for reissue) Hardcore East Coast hip hop street skate video, where Busta Rhymes, Method Man and Redman all go freestyle too

AKA: Girl Skater (Gallaz, 2002, www.girlskater.com) Documentary filmed on tour with Vanessa Torres, Jaime Reyes, Amy Caron and Monica Shaw

Breakthrough With Craig Smedley (Icon, 2002) Beginners' instruction manual with slow-mos and multiple angles taking you through over 30 tricks

Dying To Live (Zero, 2002) Handrail mayhem as Jamie Thomas takes his crew – Matt Mumford, Adrian Lopez, Chris Cole, Jon Allie et al – on a stairway to heaven. You might have to hide behind the sofa

First Broadcast (Blueprint, 2002) Riders from UK companies tear up the local streets in one of the best British skating videos for a very long time

Op King Of Skate (411VM, 2002) Bob Burnquist's $25,000-winning Loop Of Death, Tony Hawk on the Bar Of Fire, Eric Koston over the Triple Set Triple Threat, Geoff Rowley on the Ninja Night Mission, Mike Vallely over the Punk Rock Tour Buses and Danny Way's legendary two world records in one go. Phew

Sight Unseen (Transworld Skateboarding, 2002) Covers every aspect of modern skating. Plus the DVD has all the top riders explaining their parts

Wonderful Horrible Life (Colliseum Skate, 2002) Street shredding from PJ Ladd and the lads. Awesome skating, awesome soundtrack and plenty of laughs too. Out on DVD

The End (Birdhouse, 2000) Tony Hawk does loop the loop while the rest of the team – Andrew Reynolds, Steve Berra, Heath Kirchart, Jeremy Klein, Bucky Lasek, Rick McCrank and Willy Santos – do equally loopy stunts in the most expensive skate video ever. It'll make you chuckle too

Tony Hawk's Trick Tips – Skateboarding Basics (900 Films, 2000) Tony and pals Kris Markovich and Brian Sumner get you started, from buying a board to learning how to skate street, ramps, rails and ledges

Fulfill The Dream (Shorty's, 1998) Changed the course of skateboarding

Mouse (Girl, 1996) Makes you laugh. Then Eric Koston makes you cry

Welcome To Hell (Toy Machine, 1996) Another classic. Jamie Thomas, Ed Templeton, Donny Barley et al turn flip handrails and gaps to a great soundtrack featuring Pink Floyd, Iron Maiden and Black Sabbath. Has a slam section that could put you off for life

Questionable (Plan B, 1992) Legends Danny Way, Pat Duffy and Rodney Mullen at their peak. One of the first videos to feature rails

Tim & Henry's Pack Of Lies (Blind, 1992) Many pros' favourite skate video. Tim Gavin and Henry Sanchez get gnarly on the streets

Video Days (Blind, 1991) Spike Jonze directs one of the greatest skate videos of all time. Sadly, he's now gone off to Hollywood. Jackson 5,

John Coltrane and Dinosaur Jr provide the tuneage

Shackle Me Not (H-Street, 1988) Cameos from Matt Hensley, Danny Way and Sean Sheffey when they were spring chickens

Wheels Of Fire (Santa Cruz, 1987) Jaw-dropping parts from Christian Hosoi and Natas Kaupas, who pushed street skating further than ever before

The Search For Animal Chin (Powell Peralta, 1986) The usual Bones Brigade suspects scour the world looking for legendary skater Animal Chin in a vid that's gone down in folklore

 **FEATURE FILMS**

Lords Of Dogtown (2003) Feature film version of *Dogtown and Z-Boys* written by Stacy Peralta and directed by Limp Bizkit's Fred Durst, starring contemporary pro skaters

Dogtown and Z-Boys (2001) Stacy Peralta's documentary of the Zephyr team that revolutionised skateboarding in the '70s. Archive footage of Jay Adams, Tony Alva and Tony Hawk. You'll never look at a swimming pool in the same way again

The Skateboard Kid (1994) Our hero has a magic board – but he still falls off quite a bit

Gleaming The Cube (1989) Tony Hawk, Rodney Mullen and Natas Kaupas had done everything in skateboarding, so they decided to try acting. Stars Christian Slater

Back To The Future (1985) Michael J Fox inspired thousands of kids to take up skateboarding in the '80s after the street sequence at the start of this blockbuster

Wheels On Meals (1984) Kung fu hero Jackie Chan turns his talents to skateboarding

★

SOUNDS

Music has always been a big part of skatebarding – it's just another form of self-expression. As skating has grown up, it's been linked with various types of music, such as heavy metal, punk, hip hop, drum'n'bass and skate metal. Some dudes even get turned on by jazz, funk and classical music. Pro skaters have used all of these styles to soundtrack their video parts. This is a track listing for a pretty sick skate CD. But that's not to say you should start downloading straightaway. Just listen to whatever makes you get on a board and ride. Like skating, everyone has their own style. Find yours.

the best skating a
in the world...eve

SKATING THE WEB

www.skateboardmusic.com Heard a sick choon on a skateboarding vid? Find out what it is here. And then buy it. Genius

www.skaterock.com Top US music and skating site. Reviews of new bands, articles and interviews with skate stars, plus the essential A-Z of classic skate bands

> *"I listen to garage, R&B, hip hop, even jazz sometimes. It's whatever I'm in the mood for, whatever catches my ear. I don't like the stereotype people put on skating – you don't have to listen to rock music."*
> *Ross McGouran, 15, Vans Grom*

the best skating album in the world...ever

Slayer *Epidemic*
Alice Cooper *Feed My Frankenstein*
Suicidal Tendencies *Institutionalized*
Black Flag *Six Pack*
Korn *Lowrider*
Isaac Hayes *Shaft*
Beastie Boys *Sabotage*
Public Enemy *Don't Believe The Hype*
A Tribe Called Quest *Can I Kick It?*
Jungle Brothers *Moving Along*
Jackson 5 *I Want You Back*
Run DMC/Aerosmith *Walk This Way*
Lard *Self-Inflicted Pain*
OPM *Heaven Is A halfpipe*
Pennywise *Land Of The Free*
Milk *The Knife Song*
Green Day *When I Come Around*
Ned's Atomic Dustbin *Grey Cell Green*
The Streets *Weak Become Heroes*
Nirvana *Smells Like Teen Spirit*

MAGS
UK

DOCUMENT

Started up in 1999 as the first serious rival to *Sidewalk* and is an equally thumping read. Doesn't moan on about how rubbish the British weather is all the time, which is a breath of fresh – note, not freezing – air. Superb photos and information on UK skate scene.

www.4130.com/document/

KINGPIN (SKATEBOARDING EUROPA)

Aiming to unite the European skate scene, new rag *Kingpin* must be Tony Blair's favourite mag. Nice balance of serious articles and humour in various languages. Use it to work out where to go for your summer hols.

www.kingpinmag.com

SIDEWALK

Despite its name, *Sidewalk* is very British. There's gossip and park news, interviews and features on UK pros and tours, sequences from local skate spots and even music reviews. *Pavement* just wouldn't have sounded so good.
www.network26.com/Sidewalk/sidewalkhome

USA

411VM (VIDEO MAGAZINE)

A video, sure, but it is marketed as a mag, comes out monthly and contains all the same sections you'd find in *Transworld* – Pro Files, Wheels of Fortune (interviews with ams), contests, road trips, trick tips, Metrospectives (urban spot checks) and plenty of ads. It's kinder to the rainforests and easier to slow-mo.
www.411vm.com

BIG BROTHER

Nothing to do with chickens or reality TV, but a skate mag that's the printed equivalent of *Jackass*, ie stoopid stunts in stoopid costumes and a total disregard for human life. Would probably throw itself off a 15-stair rail if it ever took itself too seriously.
www.bigbrothermagazine.com

SKATEBOARDER MAGAZINE

Well written and informative with great photos, this is the kind of magazine your mum or dad wouldn't mind buying for you. Which doesn't mean it's rubbish. It's just a bit more grown-up, like.
www.skateboardermag.com

SLAP

The first issue was printed on loo paper in 1992 and was hilarious if kinda embarrassing to read on the bus. These days, *Slap* has, er, cleaned up its act, but is still funny and more popular than ever, possibly because it's now printed on real paper.

www.slapmagazine.com

THRASHER

Gave skateboarding some serious attitude when it came out in 1981 and is still giving it attitude 20 years later. *Thrasher* showcases America's craziest skaters as well as heavily featuring US underground rock music. Not very popular with old ladies.

www.thrashermagazine.com

TRANSWORLD SKATEBOARDING

The undisputed king of skateboard magazines and purveyor of awesome videos. Lots of thick, glossy pages packed with cool articles and full-on photos mean this skate bible is read all over the world. Maybe that's 'cos you can buy it in Smith's.

www.skateboarding.com

GAMES

It never rains in cyberspace. So get on a virtual board and pull off tricks that you could only dream about in real life. Plus, the only injuries you're likely to pick up are blisters on your poor fingers.

720 One of the first skating games ever, this classic mid-'80s

Atari game has been re-released

MTV Sports: Skateboarding Featuring Andy Macdonald.
The Vert Vet takes us higher

Simpsons Skateboarding Bart, Homer and Lucy shred
Springfield

Tony Hawk Pro Skater 4 The latest in the series. US parks
and spots digitally recreated for you to tear them up as
Chad Muska, Bob Burnquist, Andrew Reynolds or Tone
himself

Top Skater Cult 1997 arcade game from Sega

Transworld Skateboarding It's all about creativity and
style as pros like Danny Way and Mike Vallely are brought
to life in 10 skate spots around the globe

Amped Tired of skateboarding? Try snowboarding
instead. It's softer when you land

*"I suck at Pro Skater. Tony and I were at the
video game trade show and they asked us to
play in front of the kids and I was so
embarrassed I stopped playing. I have a
rabbit and she ate through my PlayStation
cord, so I can't play right now."*
Chad Muska, pro skater and character in Pro Skater

*"My mate and I bought the first Pro Skater
game and that got us into skateboarding
two years ago. Now I have my own skate
company, East Coast Skating."*
Wesley Lisle, 17, Great Yarmouth

chapter nineteen
Skate outta here

So now you can skateboard. Don't just think you can sit back and twiddle your toes. There's a whole world of other board sports just waiting to be conquered. What about longboarding? Or carveboarding. Or mountainboarding. Or grassboarding, sandboarding, snowboarding, surfboarding, wakeboarding, freeboarding, snakeboarding, skootboarding, skimboarding . . . Still bored? Why not try wheelbarrow freestyle (don't ask)? You can even skate on snow these days. Burton has developed the Junkyard Snowdeck. It has a skateboard deck over a mini snowboard subdeck, separated by special trucks. But best of all, there are no foot bindings, so you can take every one of your favourite skateboard tricks on to the slopes.

Look, don't get us wrong, we're not saying you should

stop skateboarding for a second. Far from it. We're just trying to keep challenging you. Once you can skate, all the other board sports should come easy. Plus they'll all help you in various ways with your skating. However good you get, there's always more to learn. Skateboarding's never-ending and that's the beauty of it.

GO FIGURE

www.angelfire.com/wv/carve Carveboarding
www.downhillskateboarding.com Downhill skateboarding
www.wakeboard.co.uk Wakeboarding
www.sandboard.com Sandboarding
www.wheelbarrowfreestyle.com Er, wheelbarrow freestyle

"A new world has opened up through skateboarding – new friends, new cities and tons of experiences. Skateboarding has helped me to understand people and taught me to question them at the same time. Skateboarding is a form of motivation, persistence, innovation and expression. It's a quest to better yourself, expand limitations and develop yourself. I will always love it for that."

Nic Patterson, 18, USA

glossary

ɴOu whəʈ?

Skating terms explained so you don't come across like a bin liner at the burger circus. If you know what I mean.

Air What you get when you fly off the top of a ramp

Airwalk Vert trick where the front foot is kicked forward and the back foot kicked back in mid-air

Alley-oop Vert trick where the body spins the opposite way to the direction of the trick

Aluminium pedaller Someone who rides a scooter

Bail To fall

Barge To go skate somewhere you're not supposed to

Big licks Speed

Big ups Respect

Bin liner Inline skater

Blunt Trick where the board ends up vertical with the rear wheels on top of an obstacle

Body varial You spin but your board doesn't

Boneless No, not how you'll be at the end of your skateboarding career. It's a kind of *no-comply* at the top of a ramp

Bongo A fall on your head

Burger Bad bruise

Burger circus Dangerous place to skate

Busting Skating well

Casper A trick that involves the underside of your board. What will we think of next? Standing on the edges? Oh, see *rail*

Catch To stop the board turning by landing on it with your feet in mid-air

Coping Grindable or slideable metal piping at the top of ramps and spines

Curb crawling To search for a good skate spot

Darkside The underside of your deck. If you keep landing darkside, Houston we have a problem

Disaster Ramp trick where your rear wheels are on the top, the middle of your deck is on the coping, and the nose is hanging off the edge

Dope Good

Dudes Your skateboard gang

Eat dirt To fall off

Flip Where the board rotates so that you can see the underside

Focus To snap your board in two. Not advisable

Front To make something up

Funbox A four-sided launch ramp

Gap Something to ollie over, like a space in the pavement. Or the Mersey

Gnarly Cool or dangerous

Graphics The design on the underside of your deck

Grindbox A wooden box found in skateparks with four metal edges for grinds and slides

Grommet You, ie, the industry's name for a kid skater

Half cab A fakie 180 ollie. Not an unlicensed taxi

Hang up To catch your back wheels on the coping as you re-enter a vert ramp. Also known as Lock

Hanger Part of the truck that you grind on

Hardflip Combination of a kickflip and a frontside 180 pop shovit

Hip The junction where two angled ramps join. For doing tricks over

Homies Your skateboard gang

Ill Good. Like *sick*, obviously

Jam A skating get-together

Kevs Townies

Kicktail The raised bit on your tail that you kick down to do an ollie

Kingpin Bolt that holds your trucks together. Liable to snap but cheap to replace

Kink Change in angle of a handrail

Lame Rubbish

Land To complete a trick

Lines Not what your teacher gives you, but riding routes through a skatepark

Lip The top edge of a ramp

Nail To get a trick just right

No-comply Old skool move where you put your front foot on the ground to do a trick

Nose Front of the board. Not the snot tap on your face

Phat Very cool, a trick that's particularly large or high

Played out Out of fashion

Pop To hit the kicktail down to start a trick. Or the amount of spring in your board

Primo When your board's on its side

Puppy Trick. As in, "Land that puppy"

Pyramid Invented by the Eygptians. Wooden box in skateparks with a flat top used for tricks (also known as a *funbox*)

Quarterpipe Half a halfpipe

Rail Side edge of your skateboard. Or a trick that involves standing on the edge of your board. Or a metal bar used for performing tricks

Revert When you and your board turn 180 degrees at the last minute as you land a trick

Rip To conquer a skate spot

Ripper A really good skater

Road rash Grazes or cuts from boarding. See also *street pizza*

Roll-in A smooth, round drop-in on a ramp

Sex change Body varial in the middle of a trick

Shred sled Your skateboard

Shred the streets To board through town

Sick Cool

Sketchy Dodgy, just about pulling off tricks but with no style

Skid lid Your helmet

Slam A hard fall

Slam time Whoops, you've just fallen off

Slick Plastic coating under the deck to help you slide. Not that you need it of course. Oh no

Snake Someone who jumps the queue at skateparks

Sound Reliable

Spear-footed Pushing mongo. You look like a Zulu warrior, fool

Spin Where the board rotates so that the nose and tail swap positions

Spine When two ramps are back to back, the top bit that sticks up in the air is the spine

Spot Anywhere that's good for skating. The best spot of course is your imagination

Stick Your board

Stoked Somewhat chuffed

Street pizza Not a welcome sidewalk snack, but grazes or cuts from skating

Swellbow When you bang your elbow and it balloons in size

Switch Riding or doing tricks with your weaker foot forward

Tail Back of the board. Or something your dog wags when you pull off a sick trick

Take a beating When you fall off a lot

Thrashed What you've done to the benches in your local park (or your own board) by grinding and sliding on them

Throw Down To skate well. And if you throw down the hammers, you're skating even better

Transfer To skate from one ramp to another

Transition Any surface that's not flat or vertical like the curved bit of a ramp. Also known as a tranny

Tweak To add your own style to a trick

Vertisis Affliction whereby vert skaters are lame at street

Wack Rubbish, pants

Wallride Skating on, yup you guessed it, a wall

Who's the man? You, after you've nailed that cool trick

appendix
Shops and Websites

You're never more than a few pushes away from your local skate shop (you can also get gear from all the indoor skateparks, see Chapter 10).

ABERDEEN Boarderline, 15 McCombies Court, 01224 626996

AMBLESIDE Sport Extreme, 5 Lake Road, 01539 432752

BANBURY Radikal, 57 George Street, 01295 709719

BANGOR D88, 68 High Street, 01248 364111

BARROW IN FURNESS Kates Skates, 12-22 Dalkeith Street, 0800 917 3027, www.katesskates.co.uk

BASILDON Limit, Upper Galleries, Eastgate Shopping Centre

BASINGSTOKE Off Beat Sportz Ltd, 01256 461960, www.offbeatsportz.co.uk

BATH Darkotics, 13 London Street, Walcot, 01225 471998

BEDFORD Planet Clothing, 18 The Arcade, 2 Clair Court, 01234 217171

BELFAST Point Seven 5ive, 31 Queen Street, 028 9031 9465

BIDEFORD Freebird, 8 The Quay, 01237 470791

BIRMINGHAM Ideal, 175 Corporation Street, 0121 236 9300

BISHOP'S STORTFORD Boomerang, 4 Florence Walk, 01279 466485

BLACKPOOL Big Woodys Skate Shop, 54a Hardhorn Road, Brimelows Garage Buildings, Poulton-le-Fylde, 01253 896030

BOURNEMOUTH The Source, 204 Old Christchurch Road, 01202 299590, www.thesource-uk.com

BRACKNELL Foxy's Skateboarding, 85 Broadway, Service Yard G, 01344 360777

BRADFORD Rocks Off, 85 Westgate, 01274 736292

BRIDGEND Bad Habits, 15 Market Street, 01656 652916

BRIDGWATER Hustlaz, 2 Court Street, 01278 444343

BRIDPORT Steptoes, East Street, 01308 421242

BRIGHTON Fat Mamas, 15 Sydney Street, 01273 685110, www.fatmamas.co.uk

BRISTOL Fifty Fifty, 16 Park Row, 0117 914 7783, www.5050skateboardsupplies.co.uk

BROMLEY Urban Chaos, 19-23 Masons Hill, 020 8460 4456, www.urban-chaos.co.uk

BUDE Airculture, Swiss Cottage, Belle Vue, 01288 356779, www.airculture.co.uk

BURNLEY East Village, 5 Yorkshire Street, 01282 835474

BURY ST EDMUNDS Hardcore Hobbies, 35 St Johns Street, 01284 717100

CAMBRIDGE Two Seasons, 34 Chesterton Road, 01223 356207, www.twoseasons.co.uk

CAMBRIDGE Billy's, 307 Mill Road, 01223 5568368

CANNOCK Boardwise, 20 Cross Street, Bridgtown, 01543 505084, www.boardwise.com

CANTERBURY Nation, Unit 2, 4-6 Orange Street, 01227 785182

CARDIFF City Surf & Skate, 27 Castle Arcade, 02920 342068

CARLISLE S4, 2 Lowther Arcade, 01228 595815

CARMARTHEN Rail 2 Grail, Unit 1, Jacksons Lane, 01267 237521

CHELMSFORD Whaam, 2 Market Road, 01245 359252

CHELTENHAM Air Circus, 18 Winchcombe Street, 01242 255411

CHESTER Legends Surf Shop, 9 Newgate Row, Grosvenor Centre, 01244 345939

CHESTERFIELD Pie Skate Store, 4 Falcon Yard, Lower Pavement, 01246 551656

COLCHESTER Hoax, 36 Eld Lane, www.hoaxskate.co.uk

COLERAINE Hideaway, 1a Hawthorne Terrace, Bushmills Road, Co Londonderry, 07870 462837

CONWAY A&E, 5 Reform Street, Llandudno, 01492 872972

COVENTRY Ride, 6 Holbrooks, 02476 681102

CRAWLEY Oddballs, 12 Broadwalk, 01293 551736

CROYDON Ollie's, 2 St George's Walk, 020 8667 1179

DERBY Rollersnakes, Breadsall Island, Alfreton Road, 0845 130 0666, www.rollersnakes.co.uk

DERBY The Curve, 40 Sadlergate, 01332 343405

DONCASTER Extreme, 86 East Laith Gate, 01302 738388

DORKING Hi-Life, 290 High Street, 01306 881910

DUBLIN Ramp N Rail Skatepark, 96a Upper Drumcondra Road, Unit 3,
Whitehall Works, 00353 01837 7533

DUDLEY Jedi Skateboarding, 90 High Street, 01384 459686,
www.jediskateboarding.co.uk

DUNDEE Effective Edge, 212a Perth Road, 01382 221155,
www.effectiveedge.co.uk

DURHAM Area 51, 53 North Road, 0191 386 2252

EDINBURGH Focus, 44 West Port, 0131 229 9009,
www.focuspocus.co.uk

ELGIN ESP, 5 Moss Street, 01343 550129

EXETER The Boarding House, 132 Fore Street, 01392 21774

FALMOUTH Freeriders, 15b, Killigrew Street, 01326 313456

FARNBOROUGH Swivel Skateshop, 44 Cove Road, 01252 517206

FARNHAM Curb Surfers, 11 Upper Church Lane, 01252 711191

FROME High Rider, 13 Catherine Hill, 01373 453727

GLASGOW Clan, 45 Hyndland Road, Partick, 0141 339 6523

GLASGOW Tribal Junki, 8 Wilson Street, Merchant City, 0141 552 7078

GREAT YARMOUTH TT Sk8's, 90 High Street, 01493 668866

GUILDFORD Ollies, 4 Phoenix Court, 01483 566626

HALESWORTH Black & White Skateboarding, Rear Unit, The Hawk, Bridge Street, 01986 875754, www.bandwskate.com

HARLOW Big Worms, 78c Harvey Centre, 01279 425067

HARROW New Deal Skates, Unit D2/3, Phoenix Industrial Estate, Rosslyn Crescent, 020 8427 2812

HARTLEPOOL Kerb Skate Store, 50 Murrey Street, 01429 262420

HAYWARDS HEATH Ballyhoo, 1 Sydney Road, Commercial Square, 01444 417805

HEREFORD Flipped, 208 Commercial Road, 01432 266361

HIGH WYCOMBE Bucks Boarding Centre, 3 Castle Street, 01494 472000, www.bucksboarding.co.uk

HITCHIN Custom Riders, 55 Bancroft, 01462 437035

HORSHAM Individual Skate Store, 20 Queen Street, 01403 264100

HUDDERSFIELD Wisdom, 8 Market Avenue, 01484 511115

HULL Four Down, Units 16-17, Paragon Arcade, Paragon Street, 01482 224976

HULL Rock City, Top Deck, Princes Quay, 01482 210599

HUNTINGDON Heshe, 9 All Saints Passage, 01480 459009

INVERNESS North 57, 51 Church Street, 01463 710960

IPSWICH Hoax, 7 St Nicholas Street, 01473 211851

ISLE OF MAN Endless Summer, 20 Duke Street, Douglas, 01624 616987

KENDAL Kendal Survival Shop, Kent View, Waterside, 01539 729699

KESWICK The Sick And The Wrong, 68 Main Street, 01768 773035

KIDDERMINSTER Dai Leisure, bottom of Comberton Hill, 01384 265151, www.daileisure.com

LANCASTER Blue Tubes, 67 King Street, 01524 32068

LEAMINGTON SPA Legends, 19-21 The Parade, Priors Gate, 01926 887717, www.legendsextreme.com

LEEDS Wisdom, 7 Crown Street, 0113 244 9129

LEICESTER Casino, 22 Malcolm Arcade, 0116 251 6362, www.casinoskates.com

LEIGH Ratcliffes, 113a Bradshawgate, 0800 214392, www.ratcliffesofleigh.co.uk

LETCHWORTH Random, Unit 5a, Market Hall, Commerce Way, 01462 675204, www.randomskatesupplies.com

LICHFIELD Old Skool, 10 Dam Street, 01543 411899

LINCOLN S3, 264 High Street, 01522 569381

LIVERPOOL Flea Pit, 12-16 School Lane, 01517 092797

LONDON Quiksilver, Thomas Neal Centre, Earlham Street, Covent Garden, 020 7836 5371

LONDON Skate Of Mind, 4 Marlborough Court, off Carnaby Street, 020 7434 0295; Unit 26, Thomas Neal Centre, Earlham Street, Covent Garden, 020 7836 9060

LONDON Slam City Skates, 16 Neal's Yard, Covent Garden, 020 7240 0928, www.slamcity.com

LOUGHBOROUGH The Rush, 13 The Rushes, 01509 231008

LURGAN Colin Senior Sports, 47 Market Street, Co Armagh, 028 3832 6128

MAIDENHEAD Hard Edge, 100 High Street, 01628 776025

MAIDSTONE Cult Skates, 27 Pudding Lane, 01622 679996, www.cultskates.co.uk

MANCHESTER Wisdom, Unit 4, 26-52 Oldham Street, Afflecks Arcade, 0161 832 3192

MANSFIELD Nonstop 2, 36 Whitehart Street, 01623 644555

MILTON KEYNES Bucks Boarding Centre, 12 Duckworth Court, Oldbrook, 01908 540180, www.bucksboarding.co.uk

NEWCASTLE NSC, 16 Shakespeare Street, 0191 230 2595

NEWMARKET Go Extreme, 10a Old Station Road, 01638 561065

NEWPORT Freestyle Skate Store, 01633 213129, www.freestyleskates.co.uk

NEWQUAY Flavour, 6 Beach Road, 01637 850515

NORTHAMPTON Two Seasons, 229-231, Wellingborough Road, 01604 627377

NORWICH Revolutionz, 25 Timber Hill, 01603 629313, www.revolutionz.co.uk

NOTTINGHAM Peak Performance, 20 St James' Street, 01159 502540, www.peakperf.co.uk

NUNEATON JR Skatestore.com, 84 Queens Road

OXFORD SS20, 131 Cowley Road, 01865 791851, www.ss20.com

PAIGNTON Vert, 7 Hyde Road, 01803 554164

PENZANCE South Shore, Unit 13, Wharfside Shopping Centre, 01736 365757, www.southshoresurfandskate.co.uk

PERTH Easy Rider, 190 South Street, 01738 451666

PERTH Woody's Skate Shack, 234 High Street, Perthshire, 01738 630033

PETERBOROUGH Rebel, 2 Park Road, 01733 319144

PLYMOUTH Flatspot, 10 Whimple Street, 01752 222213, www.flatspot.com

POOLE The Skate Shop, 115 Parkstone Road, 01202 743000

PORTSMOUTH Bored Ltd, Elm Grove, Southsea, 02392 426388

PORTSMOUTH Route One, 8 Palmerston Road, Southsea, 02392 851007

PRESTON Scene Skate Store, 47 Friargate, 01772 556412,
www.scenepreston.co.uk

READING Hard Edge, 25 Queen Victoria Street, 0118 958 4063

READING Halfpipe Sports, 385 Reading Road, Winnersh, 0118 978 1022

RUGBY Exposure, 3 St Matthew Street, 01788 541321

ST ALBANS Conspiracy, 4 Canberra House, 17 London Road, 01727 853153, www.conspiracyskateboards.com

SCARBOROUGH Secret Spot Surf Shop, 4 Pavilion Terrace, 01723 500467

SCARBOROUGH Sublime, 144 St Nicholas Street, 01723 364750

SEVENOAKS Logo Merchandising, 9a London Road, 01732 462958

SHEFFIELD Five Forty, 659-661 Eccleshall Road, Hunters Bar 0114 266 0321

SHEFFIELD Sumo, 96 Devonshire Street, 0114 275 7143,
www.sumostore.com

SOUTHAMPTON Off Beat Sportz Ltd, 186 Above Bar, 02380 330600,
www.offbeatsportz.co.uk

SOUTHAMPTON Legends, The Marlands Shopping Centre, Civic Centre Road, 02380 336556, www.legendsextreme.com

STAFFORD Switch, 104b Wolverhampton Road, 01785 256202,
www.switchskateboards.com

STAMFORD Logic, St Paul's Street, 01780 762224

STIRLING The Boardroom, Unit 12, Crawford Arcade

STOCKPORT Note, Skatepark, Canal Street, 0161 429 7772

STOCKTON-ON-TEES Mischief, 5 Regency West Mall, 01642 608400,
www.mischiefskatestore.com

STOCKTON-ON-TEES Xtreme, 704 Yarm Road, Eaglescliffe,
01642 352669

STOKE-ON-TRENT Dazed, 12 Brunswick Street, Hanley, 01782 201057

SUDBURY The Blim Box, 12b King Street

SUNDERLAND Gravity Projects, 67 Villette Road, 0191 514 2266

SUNDERLAND Habit, 222 High Street West, 0191 514 1974

SUTTON COLDFIELD, One World The Store, 14a Birmingham Road, 0121 321 3535

SWANSEA City-Surf-Skate-Snow, 4 Picton Arcade, 01792 654169

SWINDON Just Add Water, 18 The Arcade, 01793 496345, www.justaddwatersports.co.uk

SWINDON Tower 12, 96 Victoria Road, 01793 521831, www.tower12.co.uk

TAMWORTH Blend, 10 Bolebridge Mews, Bolebridge Street, 01827 60588

TORQUAY BKT, 21 Abbey Road, 01803 213185

TRURO SJ'z, 9 Saint Marys Mews, 01872 223533

TUNBRIDGE WELLS Route One, 9 Ely Court, 01892 539599

WAKEFIELD Board Riders, The Old Vicarage, Zetland Street, 01924 381300

WARRINGTON SK8FX Skatesports, 752 Knutsford Road, Latchford, 01925 656463

WATFORD RnR Skates, 39 Market Street, 01923 449191, www.rnrskates.com

WESTON-SUPER-MARE The Playground, 67 Meadow Street, 01934 418758

WIGAN Alan's, 53 Mesnes Street, 01942 826598

WINCHESTER Caned Clothing, 9a Great Minster Street, 01962 849757

WINDSOR Extreme Motion, Alexandra Gardens, Alma Road, 01753 830220, www.extrememotion.com

WOKING Surrey Skateboards.com, 27 Chertsey Road, 01483 760019

WOLVERHAMPTON Warped Sports, Unit 7, Parkside Industrial Estate, 01902 717705

WORCESTER Spine, Unit 2, The Hopmarket, 01905 23300

WORTHING Hobo Boardriders, 39 Warwick Street, 019032 32335

YORK Mayhem, 7 Jubber Gate, 01904 655062

SKATING THE WEB

www.boardsonline.co.uk, www.thedopeshop.co.uk,
www.exit.uk.com, www.extremepie.com, www.headstrong.co.uk,
www.popcornskate.co.uk

WEBSITES

www.bobburnquist.com All about the great jumping Brazilian

www.casinoskates.com Site for and run by skaters around Leicester

www.ersports.com US site covering all types of boarding with interviews, articles and mucho video action

www.exploratorium.edu/skateboarding Get top marks in physics by learning the science behind skating – like why your board sticks to your feet when you ollie. Another great reason to persuade your parents to let you skateboard – it's education, innit?

http://expn.go.com Get up to date with everything big, brash and US-shaped

www.geocities.com/sk8hull All you ever wanted to know about skating in Hull

www.hardflip.co.uk Loads of advice for beginners, a big tricks section, a list of skateparks, plus a chat forum

www.insane-riders.com Updates on new skateparks and spots, in-depth articles and reviews of products and videos, plus photos and message boards. Great for a rainy day

www.iol.ie/~owenh/freeflow The boarding scene in Dublin

www.jerseysk8.moonfruit.com The lowdown on Jersey

http://mag.monsterskate.com Skateboarding magazine with interviews with top skaters and articles on the sport, photos, videos, shopping, you name it

www.sheffieldsk8in.cjb.net, **www.sk8porn.cjb.net** & **www.safewaymob.co.uk** That's Sheffield sorted then

www.skateboarddirectory.com List of all major US skateboard sites, including board, equipment and clothing companies

www.skateboarding.com Transworld's site. Good tricks sections with instructional videos plus entertaining features and a chat room

www.skateboarding.nu Everything you ever wanted to know about skateboarding all over Europe. So you can plan where to go for your summer hols

www.skatepark.org All the information and help you need to persuade your council to build a skatepark in your own back yard

www.skateparkpages.co.uk List of UK skateparks, plus lots of other skate-related stuff

www.skatetalk.com Chat with your bro' in the good ole US of A

www.sketchyskateboarding.co.uk Best connected skate site on the Net – links galore

www.switchmagazine.com Name a trick and they've got it. There's even some you didn't think were physically possible. Plus excellent interviews and articles from the US

www.tonyhawk.com Check to see whether the great man is appearing near you and improve your ride by buying some of Tony's own boards and gear

www.zboys.com Loads of info and articles about the birth of modern skateboarding